Kathy,

SCANDALOUS!
HIGHWAY ROBBERY
WELLS FARGO
FALLS OFF THE WAGON

BY ALAN B. JONAS

Best,

Alan

DORRANCE
PUBLISHING CO
EST 1920
PITTSBURGH, PENNSYLVANIA 15238

Dorrance Publishing Co
585 Alpha Drive
Pittsburgh, PA 15238
Visit our website at *www.dorrancebookstore.com*

ISBN: 978-1-6495-7192-2
eISBN: 978-1-6495-7700-9

Table of Contents

ACKNOWLEDGMENTS

It couldn't have come from a better observer. Chris Forsyth, the editor of this book, in reading the preface for the first time, took his hat off to me as one of the founders of "retail banking." That was the term he used in reporting its birth and growth when he worked for ANG Newspapers—as reporter, editor, and editorial page editor of various mastheads. He authored five published books and was a speech writer for a leading Silicon Valley CEO.

When I introduced financial products to customers at banks and credit unions through The Financial Store, it was revolutionary at the time. Banks were banks in those days, pure and simple. They sold banking products to their customers and members—savings accounts and CDs. That was it. But they were looking for other ways to increase revenue just as insurance companies were seeking other avenues of income by means of teaming up with brokerage firms, à la Prudential Bache.

In January, 2020, Chris sent me the following email: "There's no sense in the world if you can't sell your book in light of these multi-million-dollar fines on Stumpf (CEO of Wells Fargo) and other Wells miscreants." It wasn't soon after that when a good friend and former business associate emailed me the following: "My God. If I did that, I'd be in jail."

I would like to acknowledge the patience and support of my family, including my daughters Mindy, Lauren, and Corinne, along with my friends who took a back seat to my writing endeavors. It's not easy taking second fiddle to a dedicated author who wanted to transcribe history in the making. Thank you to Corinne for initially acting as liaison with the publishing company. I owe Lauren tremendous gratitude for steering me through the structuring of the manuscript. She also contacted and hired artist Simon Winheld who designed the book cover in painstaking detail. Many thanks to him for taking the time out of his busy schedule to complete the task. Thank you to Mindy for many hours spent overseeing the final proofreading and editing. To her daughter and my granddaughter Elise, co-editor-in-chief of her high school's newspaper *San Marin Pony Express*, a debt of gratitude for setting up my website and its corresponding features. It must run in the family as I, too, was the editor-in-chief of a newspaper.

Lastly, my tongue-in-cheek thanks to the former CEO of Wells Fargo, John Stumpf, who made such a mockery of running a business that, without him and his outlandish behavior, I wouldn't be writing this book and the name Wells Fargo would still be attached to its wagon.

Retail Banking Is Born

The year was 1982. I was attending a conference arranged by my broker-dealer at the time. I had just co-founded The Financial Store, the only independent financial services firm to be located in a shopping center at that time. Sears had a Financial Center located in the same shopping center, but it was staffed by three salespeople all trying to sell their respective products mainly to the same customer. In effect, they were in competition with each other with little or no coordination.

At the conference, the president of the broker-dealer asked me if I would lead a discussion of how to attract new clients. I described how I was doing this not only within the shopping center environment but also trying to affiliate with local banks and credit unions. The Financial Store was located at the front of the main entrance to the shopping center and directly across the street was none other than Wells Fargo Bank. I remember ending my comments at the conference with the advice: "Join the ranks of the banks because, as Willie Sutton once said, 'That's where the money is.'"

One of the outside guest speakers to address the entire group of brokers at the conference was an employee of Wells Fargo. She described how the bank tried to attract new business from old clients. Referring to its branches as "stores," she said the bank wanted to give the image of products on the shelf waiting to be purchased. These included mutual funds, stocks and bonds, IRA's and even tax shelters. To make the branches look buyer friendly, there were desks and sofas arranged in the center of the branch. My partner and I looked at each other in amazement because this was exactly what The Financial Store would look like. We couldn't wait to return to our store to make some changes such as putting signs in our windows listing our products. We even set up a miniature store in the lobby of the shopping center, which started to attract attention from passersby. We put a box in front when we weren't there so a shopper could fill out a mini questionnaire and insert it in the box. We followed up by calling to make an appointment.

Immediately after the conference, I called an old acquaintance who had been a vice president at Wells Fargo and arranged for a meeting. I told him about the woman at the conference and how she referred to her branches as "stores." I told him about The Financial Store and he became very excited about the concept and wanted to know how I came up with the name. His next question was "What are you selling in the store?" When I told him we first start out with a financial plan, which then can lead to investments and product sales, he became quite agitated and started to yell at me. "Why a financial plan? Why don't you eliminate that and go right to the sale of products?" I was quite taken aback and didn't know how to respond. The meeting ended abruptly and so I left.

A few weeks later, he called me and offered this proposition: "You can set up your stores in our branches but for product sales only, not financial plans." He said he would have a vice president call me to work out the details. A vice president from the LA area flew up to San Francisco where we met. But there was a "but" and a big one at that. He wanted me to open up the stores in his branches in Southern California starting in the LA area. I wanted to start in the Bay Area because that's where I knew brokers and that's where I lived. As a result, the deal fell through and I looked for another bank.

Through another acquaintance, I was introduced to Union Bank where I met with a vice president who was captivated by the idea. After several meetings with bank officials, my partner and I visited a few branches in San Francisco to select the ones in which we would begin.

We were all set to start the hiring process when a second bombshell hit. Union Bank was acquired by a Japanese bank that nixed the deal. It wanted to sell banking products and not investments.

So, for Alan and partner, we had to find another source of expanding our stores and sought out credit unions. After a year, we were located in seven credit unions and one bank in California and Texas. We held seminars in the branches and eventually our business consisted mostly of tax-deferred annuities because of the conservative nature of the credit unions' members and the tax-deferral, which the savings accounts and CD's didn't offer.

The former vice president at Wells Fargo contacted me to announce he was now at Bank of America and wanted to know if I wanted to put The Financial Store in its branches in the Seattle area where he was located and, if so, how soon could I hire the necessary corps of brokers. When I explained that it wasn't easy to find qualified personnel, he didn't understand why it would be a problem. But I knew from my experience as a branch manager, it would be an arduous task of trying to find the right people who had an impressive track record and, most importantly, put the clients' interest first. Since we clashed in principle, the arrangement never proceeded.

But what materialized, in a much larger sale, was the implementation by all major banks to offer investment products to their customers, maybe not with the zeal that Wells Fargo did, but it changed the way banks conducted their business. It was reminiscent of the way brokerage firms sold products that they had never sold before, mainly life insurance and annuities. They've come a long way, baby.

I recall that when I started at Merrill Lynch in 1968, it wouldn't let me sell mutual funds because management thought it would interfere with the steady commissions on the sale of stocks and bonds. When all was said and done, mutual fund companies started to pay annual fees to brokerage firms that sold their funds. It wasn't the same commission that was paid to the brokers, but they were disguised as finder fees. Soon afterward, insurance companies wanted to get into the business of selling investment products and within a short period of time, insurance companies and brokerage firms started to merge— Prudential Insurance and Bache & Co., as an example, becoming Prudential Bache, which later dropped the name Bache when it was subsequently purchased by Wells Fargo's predecessor.

The expansion of investment products reminded me of when I worked at Sutro & Co., the venerable San Francisco brokerage firm. I vividly recall the sales manager calling me on the phone to congratulate me for selling the firm's first life insurance policy. He wanted to know about the circumstances and the purpose of the sale. I was subsequently promoted to a vice president and the company had me visit a few of the branches to tell the other brokers how I sold the product. It was very unusual in those days for a stockbroker to study for and take an exam to be licensed to sell life insurance. Although the selling of insurance to the public is a good idea, it's a far better idea if the insurance is appropriate and the buyer is aware of it. Not so with Wells Fargo.

A year-long investigation by the California Department of Insurance blamed the bank for the sale of nearly 1,500 unauthorized renters and term life insurance policies on "improper sales practices." These policies were sold to Wells Fargo customers at computer kiosks inside the bank's branches between 2008 and 2016. Kiosks? Even though the policies were provided by Prudential and other third parties, Wells Fargo's notoriously unrealistic sales goals counted these insurance referrals towards employee compensation goals. "Many customers complained they simply had no knowledge of ever signing up for such policies,"[1] the Department of Insurance said.

Other Wells Fargo customers said bank employees entered their information on a policy application "in the guise of merely issuing a quote, when in fact such applications were later submitted."[2] That's despite the fact that the kiosks were supposed to be "self-service" because

Wells Fargo employees weren't licensed to sell insurance. Authorities said Wells Fargo "caused" a total of 1,469 unauthorized insurance policies to be issued just to California customers. In 2017, California regulators were moving to suspend or even revoke Wells Fargo's insurance licenses after the investigation found the bank "lacking in integrity and having shown incompetency or untrustworthiness."[3] Some of the life policy applications listed obviously fake home and email addresses like "Wells Fargo Drive" or "noemail@wellsfargo.com."

"We are sorry for any harm this caused our customers," Wells Fargo said in a statement, adding that it was cooperating with California authorities. "Consumers should not be treated like chattel by corporations who take advantage of and abuse the consumers' trust," Insurance Commissioner Dave Jones said in a statement. "Companies licensed to transact business have an obligation to act with integrity, to obtain consumer consent before placing insurance, to disclose relevant and material information, and to comply with all state insurance laws."[4]

Wells Fargo said it suspended its online insurance operation in December 2016 and was "making things right"[5] for customers with refunds. But what if some or all of these customers wanted the insurance and were counting on it? And what if some of them had since died owning these policies? What then? Also, what is the thought process of these customers in buying insurance through a kiosk? I guess they were not aware of the age-old saying "Insurance is sold, not bought." In December 2016, Wells Fargo announced that it was quitting the personal insurance business except for life insurance, which it planned on keeping. Since 2003, it had sold only auto, homeowners, renters, and umbrella personal insurance.

CHAPTER 1

BREAK THE BANK? DON'T BANK ON IT

Willie Sutton was once asked why he continually robbed banks. He reportedly answered: "Because that's where the money is." If he were alive today, he might have second thoughts. The way many banks have been "stealing," one gets the impression they won't have any money left for robbers to get their hands on after paying those hefty fines and penalties. But they keep raking in the dough so there's plenty left over after shelling out all that moolah.

Following is the amount of fines and penalties the six largest U.S. banks (ranked by assets in 2017) were forced to pay due to their mischievous actions from 2003 through 2016. Wells Fargo earned the dubious distinction of ranking fourth among the top Most Complained About Companies with 16,146. The top three were not banks but credit reporting companies that suffered a serious securities breach.

JP MORGAN CHASE

2009 – settled with the Securities Exchange Commission (SEC) for $75 million in fines and $647 million in disclaimed fees over allegedly bribing officials in Jefferson County, Alabama.

2010 – agreed to a $6 billion settlement with the Federal Deposit Insurance Corporation (FDIC) and $208 million in a class-action settlement over disputes dealing with its purchase of Washington Mutual.

2011 – agreed to pay a combination of fines and mortgage relief of $5.3 billion over a fraud scheme that affected millions of homeowners.

2011 – settled a class action lawsuit for $100 million over allegations that it tricked credit card customers into higher fees and interest rates.

2012 – settled with the SEC for $297 million over allegedly misleading investors.

2012 – settled for $100 million with the Comptroller of the Currency, the Federal Reserve and the Commodity Futures Trading Commission (CFTC).

2012 – agreed to pay more than $300 million to about 750,000 mortgage borrowers for its forced placed insurance practices.

2012 – fined $20 million plus forced to refund $309 million in fees by the Consumer Financial Protection Bureau (CFPB) over allegedly illegal credit card practices.

2012 – paid $4.5 billion to settle yet another class-action lawsuit over allegedly misleading investors.

2013 – agreed to a $13 billion settlement with the Justice Department over allegations of mortgage and securities fraud connected with the financial crisis of 2007–2009.

2013 – fined $108 million over allegedly rigging the LIBOR inter-bank interest rate.

2013 – agreed to a $1.7 billion settlement with the Department of Justice over allegedly enabling Bernie Madoff's Ponzi scheme.

2014 – fined $350 million by the Office of The Controller of The Currency (OCC) for rigging the foreign exchange market.

2014 – fined $352 million by the British Financial Conduct Authority (FCA) for rigging the foreign exchange market.

2014 – fined $550 million plus a felony guilty plea by the Department of Justice for rigging the foreign exchange market.

2014 – fined $310 million by the CFTC.

2015 – fined $342 million by the Federal Reserve as part of a foreign exchange scam.

2015 – fined $136 million by the CFPB, $30 million by the OCC and $50 million with the Federal Trade Commission over alleged fraud associated with the financial crisis of 2007–2009.

2015 – agreed to a $150 million settlement with the SEC over an alleged failure to disclose losses.

2015 – agreed to a $137 million settlement with the Justice Department for allegedly rigging the municipal bond market.

2015 – agreed to a $415 million settlement with the SEC and to admit wrongdoing for illegally trading with customer deposits.

TOTAL – $35.177 BILLION

Who's next in the banking fraud lineup? Let's take a look at

CITIGROUP

2010 – agreed to a $550 million settlement with the SEC over the notorious ABACUS deal, in which it allegedly colluded with trader John Paulson to create a security filled with toxic loans that Paulson could bet against, then sold it to a German bank without disclosing Paulson's involvement.

2011 – agreed to a $285 million settlement with the SEC over alleged securities fraud.

2011 – paid $158 million in a civil settlement over allegedly defrauding the government's mortgage insurance programs.

2012 – paid $590 million to settle a class-action suit over allegedly misleading investors.

2013 – paid $730 million to settle another class-action lawsuit over allegedly misleading investors.

2013 – paid 968 million to Fannie Mae to resolve claims on 3.7 million home loans that have soured or may go bad.

2013 – paid $395 million to Freddie Mac to settle flawed mortgage claims.

2015 – paid $925 million plus admitted guilt for rigging foreign exchange markets.

2015 – paid $342 million to the Federal Reserve for rigging foreign exchange markets.

2015 – fined $700 million by the CFPB over allegedly illegal credit card practices.

2015 – fined $175 million by the CFTC for allegedly rigging two key inter-bank Interest rate benchmarks.

TOTAL – $8.518 BILLION

BANK OF AMERICA

(including Countrywide and Merrill Lynch)

2010 – agreed to a $108 million settlement with the Federal Trade Commission over alleged fraud associated with the financial crisis of 2007–2009.

2010 – agreed to a $150 million settlement with the SEC over an alleged failure to disclose losses.

2010 – agreed to a $137 million settlement with the Justice Department for allegedly rigging the municipal bond market.

2011 – paid $315 million to settle a class-action lawsuit over allegedly misleading investors.

2011 – agreed to a $335 million settlement with the Justice Department over alleged lending discrimination by a bank it had bought.

2011 – settled with Fannie Mae and Freddie Mac for $2.8 billion over allegedly selling faulty loans.

2012 – paid $2.43 billion to settle another class action lawsuit about allegedly misleading investors.

2013 – settled for $165 million with the National Credit Union Administration (NCUA) over alleged bad loans.

2013 – agreed to a $131 million SEC settlement over allegedly misleading investors.

2013 – paid $3.6 billion over alleged mortgage and securities fraud connected with the financial crisis of 2007–2009.

2014 – agreed to pay $16 billion for mortgage fraud, the largest settlement on record; homeowners to get $7 billion.

2016 – agreed to a $415 million SEC settlement and to admit wrongdoing for illegally trading with customer deposits.

TOTAL – $ 26.586 BILLION

WELLS FARGO

2009 – agreed to buy back $1.4 billion in mortgage securities in a settlement with California over allegedly misleading investors.

2010 – agreed to provide $2 billion more in relief to California.

2011 –   agreed to a $148 million settlement with the Justice Department over alleged municipal bond rigging done by a bank it had bought (to which was added $37 million settlement on Wells Fargo itself).

2011 –   paid $125 million to settle a class-action lawsuit over allegedly misleading investors.

2012 –   agreed to a $175 million settlement with the Justice Department over allegedly racist lending practices.

2013 –   agreed to pay Freddie Mac $869 million over allegedly bad loans.

2016 –   agreed to a $1.2 billion settlement with the Justice Department over allegedly illegal mortgage lending.

2016 –   fined $100 million by the Department of Justice.

2016 –   fined $264 million by the SEC.

2016 –   fined $61 million by the Federal Reserve.

2018 –   agreed to pay $575 million to resolve state and D.C. investigations.

2019 –   agreed to pay California $5 million to settle allegations that it issued about 1,500 insurance policies to its customers and charged them without their consent. It also agreed to forfeit its insurance licenses for two years and to pay another $5 million if it wants to sell insurance in California again.

2020 –   fined $3 billion by the United States Treasury, $500 million of which paid to the SEC (Securities Exchange Commission).

Listed below are the types and amounts of penalties submitted by the CFPB 2000–2018. It ranked fourth in the top 20 Most Complained About Companies in those years.

Mortgage abuses -	$5,576,500,000
Banking violations -	$2,966,932,386
Toxic securities abuses -	$1,530,500,000
False Claims Act -	$1,200,000,000[*]
Consumer protection violation -	$534,800,000
Wage and hour violation -	$205,403,723

Anti-money laundering deficiencies -	$163,500,000
Securities issuance or trading violation -	$155,724,464
Price-fixing or anti-competitive practices -	$148,000,000
Investor protection violation -	$38,072,000

* A federal law that imposes liability on persons and companies who defraud governmental programs.

TOTAL - $21.539 BILLION

GOLDMAN SACHS

2016 – agreed to the largest regulatory penalty in its history by paying more than $5 billion to U.S. and states stemming from the sale of mortgage bonds between 2005 and 2007. The Justice Department charged that it had misrepresented mortgage-backed securities.

TOTAL - $5.0 BILLION

MORGAN STANLEY

2003 – along with nine other brokerage firms, agreed to settle enforcement actions by the SEC pertaining to research analyst conflicts of interest from at least July, 1999 through June, 2001. It also settled civil and regulatory actions brought by the Securities Division of the Commonwealth of Massachusetts, the SEC, the NYSE and FINRA (Financial Industry Regulatory Authority). It paid a penalty of $25 million, restitution of $25 million and $75 million to be used for independent research.

2012 – settled with the Securities Division of the Commonwealth of Massachusetts for $5 million after its investment division inappropriately influenced research analysts. This is the same Morgan Stanley that was hired by Facebook to be its lead underwriter for its notorious IPO.

2016 – agreed to pay $2.6 billion in connection with its sale, marketing and is-suance of Residential Mortgage Backed Securities (RMBS). It acknowl-edged in writing that it failed to disclose critical information to prospective investors about the quality of the loans and about its due diligence practices. Investors, including federally insured financial in-stitutions, incurred billions of dollars in losses from investing in RMBS in 2006–2007 which led to the economic crisis in 2007 and 2008.

TOTAL – $2.725 BILLION

GRAND TOTAL – $ 91.253 BILLION

(NOT GRAND – BUT SHAMEFUL!)

CHAPTER 2

THINGS NOT GOING WELL AT WELLS

Chorus

"O-ho the Wells Fargo Wagon is a-comin' down the street,
Oh please let it be for me!
O-ho the Wells Fargo Wagon is a-comin' down the street,
I wish, I wish I knew what it could be!

"O-ho the Wells Fargo Wagon is a-comin' down the street,
Oh, don't let him pass my door!
O-ho the Wells Fargo Wagon is a-comin' down the street
I wish I knew what he was comin' for.

Young Winthrop (with a lisp)

"O-ho the Wells Fargo Wagon ith-a-comin' now,
I don't know how I can ever wait to thee.
It could be thumpin' for thumone who is
No relation but it could be thump'n thpethyul
Just for me!"

(from the Broadway musical "The Music Man")

The word "thump'n" almost rhymes with Stumpf, the once-upon-a-time CEO of Wells Fargo Bank. But I know for a fact that Meredith Willson, who wrote the music and lyrics could never have heard of Stumpf because he wasn't around at the time. But for hundreds of thousands of Wells Fargo customers, they probably were better off not hearing about him either under his watch.

Over the years, I had heard and read quite a bit about him. As a stockbroker, I encouraged some of my clients to buy Wells stock. We left off the Fargo since everyone in my business knew it was Wells the bank. Strange as it seemed then, whenever he gave a speech or spoke to brokers, he came across as stiff and formal. I just felt something was out of kilter with his demeanor and his aloofness. I couldn't put my finger on it, but boy, oh boy, did I get that right.

How could anybody, let alone the CEO of a bank, pull off such she-nanigans? Did he really think he was going to get away with them? And why were his lieutenants towing the corporate line? Did they, too, think no one would find out? And what about those hapless employees or "team members" as they were called who actually did their dirty work for fear of losing their jobs? Why did most of them stick around? We'll find out in forthcoming chapters.

Surely, there is treachery in any business. But in a bank? Every branch portrays a formal atmosphere, or tries to, which exhibits trust. After all, that's where the money is and handling one's money is sup-posed to be serious business. However, as we delve into this deceit, it will become very clear how Wells Fargo (yes, Fargo is the other half of the title) got into such a mess. What rhymes with crimes? You need look no further than Wells Fargo's 2010 annual report. In it, Chief Ex-ecutive Officer and President John Stumpf, wrote:

> *"I'm often asked why we set cross-sell goal of eight.*
> *The answer is, it rhymed with 'great.' Perhaps our*
> *new cheer should be: 'Let's go again, for 10!'"* [1]

In 2010 it was eight. It's what Wells Fargo called the "Gr-eight initiative." [2] Go again for 10? It was far more than that in subsequent years. So much so that employees were forced to endanger their customers and themselves.

In his testimony before a Congressional committee, Stumpf made it sound as though the employees who didn't play along were bad apples or lone wolves who disregarded the company's code of ethics. And what was that code? As it was later revealed, it was a code of dishonesty, fraud and the tenet that the company always comes first even if loyal customers had to suffer. It seems impossible to believe that any honest person working at Wells Fargo would have felt okay about opening fake accounts. But as social scientists Nina Mazar and Daniel Ariely have argued, "people like to think of themselves as honest." But their research shows that "people behave dishonestly enough to profit but honestly enough to delude themselves of their own integrity."[3] Wells Fargo employees may have convinced themselves they were not "stealing" because they weren't directly moving money from someone's account. They were just moving it from one account to another.[4]

As early as 2011, the Wells Fargo board was informed about reports of ethics violations but the cheating continued which resulted in the firing of at least 1,000 people per year in 2011, 2012 and 2013. Any company that fires thousands knows or should know that certain factors are contributing to the cheating. But instead of addressing those factors, the bank allowed the situation to persist. In the words of Representative Sean Duffy, who dismissed the CEO's claim that they are now "trying" to fix the problem, "We're five years on! ... I don't buy it."[5] Five years later, Wells Fargo is finally sending customers an email every time a new account is opened and the bank is revising its sales goals. It also needed to crack down on those supervisors who threatened employees over sales targets.[6]

About a year ago, I applied for and received a Wells Fargo credit card because Wells Fargo was offering a $100 bonus if I used the card and charged $500 on it within a three-month period. That was a cinch since I knew I would receive that $100 because I usually charge more than $500. Found money, I thought. But when I found out about the many Wells Fargo scandals, I tore it in half and threw it away where I thought it belonged.

On April 12, 2018, I received the following email from Wells Fargo: "As part of our commitment to make things right, we have entered into a $142 million class action settlement related to the opening of unauthorized accounts. If you believe Wells Fargo opened a checking, savings, credit card, or line of credit account for you without your permission, or if you purchased identify theft protection from us, you may be entitled to compensation from this fund. If you submit a claim, you may be eligible for reimbursement of fees, compensation for potential impact on your credit, and an additional cash payment based on any money remaining in the fund after benefits and costs are paid out. The deadline to submit a claim is July 7, 2018." The key here is how much money would be available for an additional cash payment after benefits and costs are paid out. What costs? How much are these costs?

On May 24, 2018, I received the following email from Wells Fargo: "We recently sent you an email letting you know that, as part of our commitment to make things right, Wells Fargo entered into a $142 million settlement. If you haven't yet submitted a claim in the settlement, you can do so at wfsettlement.com."

Four days later, I received the following email from Wells Fargo: "You're invited to activate this low-rate balance transfer offer of 0% APR on balance transfers for 15 months 14.49% variable APR after that. Dear Alan B. Jonas, **Take advantage of our limited-time balance transfer offer and enjoy the benefits.**"

These balance transfers are nothing new. Banks have been doing this for years. I find it curious that this should come to me AFTER the two emails about filing a claim.

I have also received emails from Wells Fargo with the following subject: "You have a Starbucks offer available. Come get your rewards!" It stated, "Elevate your day now with your favorite beverages and snacks at your nearest participating Starbucks store, and for a limited time you can earn 10% Bonus Cash Rewards on your first purchase of $5 or more on maximum purchase of $25 when you use your Wells Fargo rewards-based credit card."

Good 'ole Wells Fargo. Trying to get me to do business with them with a purported deal with Starbucks. Subsequently, offers from the Earn More Mall® site contained various bonus cash rewards from major retailers. It opened with: "Keep calm and earn. Last-minute shopping? We know the feeling. Here's your chance to polish off your gift list while earning rewards. As a *Go Far Rewards* customer (not true), shop online through the *Earn More Mall* to earn Bonus Cash Rewards with these special offers, now through 12/31/18." Many big name stores were listed where I could get discounts. They included Walmart, Home Depot, Lowe's, Kohl's, Nike and Walgreens. Too bad Wells was far less generous in the way its customers were being treated.

On October 12, 2018, I received an email with the subject: "Your car needs you. Earn now at Advance Auto Parts." Its title is "GoFar® Rewards. Think ahead. Think advance." It states I can earn "15% Bonus Cash Rewards on auto parts." The following day, I received another email notifying me I could earn extra dollars if I spent so much at a supermarket. It makes me wonder who's minding the store at the bank?

In November, 2018, I received yet another email which stated: "Holiday greetings and heartfelt thanks for being our customer. Thank you for the opportunity to help with your financial needs. We appreciate your business today and look forward to helping you reach your goals tomorrow. We're grateful to be able to serve, just as we're grateful to be able to serve our communities when they need a helping hand. We know that when our customers and communities succeed, we all succeed."

On February 22, 2019, I received the following email: "New year. New look. Continued commitment. At Wells Fargo, we are constantly seeking out ways to enhance security and help you stay online. Since this includes being careful when opening unfamiliar emails, we want you to know you'll soon start seeing communications from us that look different, including a revised logo and stagecoach (Ouch! They're going so far as updating their iconic stagecoach which has suited them well for a century and a half? What's up?). The email continues with "These updates are a small reflection of the big changes we're making across the company to better serve you – our customers. And we didn't want you to be surprised."

SURPRISED? I SURELY WAS SINCE I DIDN'T HAVE AN ACCOUNT AT WELLS FARGO.

Enough already. First the bank devises fake accounts and now it's grateful for helping with another fake account – mine! I was also complimented that because of my "overwhelming response," Wells Fargo was "building on the success of last year's food bank to again help families facing hunger. Your eagerness to help and contribute has inspired us to make it even easier. That's why we're collecting non-perishable food donations at approximately 5,700 branches and accepting monetary donations at more than 13,000 ATMs. To make my donations go further, we're matching monetary contributions to Feeding America® up to $1 million through December 31, 2018: 100% of donations will benefit Feeding America food banks across the country. We're also donating another $4 million – that's 40 million meals to Feeding America. We wish you joy during this holiday season. Once again, thank you for being our customer." I wonder what kind of a greeting I would get if they found out I wasn't their customer?

In 2011, a client of mine had an account at Wells Fargo which cost him $100 to open. He had to deposit a minimum of $25,000 to earn a fabulous 1%. He showed me the material they gave him upon opening the account. He thought he was earning 15.20% but that was the APR for late payments for the first six months. After that, it would be 22.15%. He misinterpreted this to mean that this would be the interest rate he would be earning. When he showed me the material, I went to the bank to make sure I understood this. After speaking to four employees who couldn't answer my questions, I demanded they close the account and refund his $100. My client didn't care about the $100. He just wanted to get out of the mess.

Bank of America was censored doing the same thing and had to pay a hefty fine plus refund the fees collected because it didn't log in payments that came in before their due date, but delayed crediting the payment until after the due date so it could collect the late payment penalties. These banks seem to follow one another in cheating their customers, especially since the Dodd-Frank regulations dramatically reduced the ways they can collect fees.

Two other clients of mine, husband and wife, had a joint tenancy account at Wells Fargo. After I helped them establish a living trust, I instructed them to go to their local branch to transfer their stock account to a new account in the name of their trust. A few weeks later, when their monthly statement was generated, I noticed that their account was still in joint tenancy. I told them to go back to the branch, speak to the branch manager and get it straightened out. They said the manager told them the new title didn't have to be on their statement, that the back office had a record of their trust so all was up to date. Not so fast. I told them to call the main office and make sure their next statement showed the new title. This went on for three more months, so I advised them to transfer their account to another bank. They wanted to wait another month. In the meantime, they spoke to the manager again and let him know that if the next statement didn't have the new title, they were going to transfer their account to another bank. The new title did appear after four months. Very frustrating to say the least.

The same couple had to change their accounts twice—once due to a successful phishing attempt against the City of Sausalito, CA which resulted in their sending their W-2. Six months later, they caught a bogus online account set up in the wife's name. If she had not been diligent, it could have become much worse. And then again, someone attempted to pass off an electronically doctored check on the new account in Florida.

Luckily, she told me, Wells now has a Fraud Detection Agency, which called her. She was advised to change their account yet again, and she told them she would not because changing the many auto transfers was a nightmare. She was told they could legally close their account if they didn't change it and that they would be held financially responsible for any damages. It turns out they lied to her, according to their agent at IDTheftSmart. What they told her as related to me was a violation of the Electronic Transfer Fund Act. Whew!

In the late 1940s, there was a popular radio show called "The Pause That Refreshes" featuring Jane Froman, a popular singer at that time. I attended many of those broadcasts. They were free to the public as its sponsor Coca Cola wanted to get many people into the theatre. Fast forward to 2018. Probably without knowing it, Wells Fargo wanted to take a pause that it hoped would refresh, too. But what came out was not a broadcast but, instead, hypocrisy.

A News Release dated March 1, 2018, was titled "Wells Fargo Board Refreshment Continues. Chen, Dean, Hernandez and Pena to retire at 2018 Annual Meeting of Shareholders." It stated: "In continuation of the board refreshment process begun in 2017, Wells Fargo & Company announced today that John S. Chen, Lloyd H. Dean, and Enrique Hernandez, Jr., currently the board's longest serving directors, and Federico F. Pena, who was scheduled to retire from the board in 2019, have decided to retire at the company's 2018 Annual Meeting of Shareholders.

"On behalf of the entire board, I want to thank John, Lloyd, Rick, and Federico for their many contributions and service to our board and company," said Board Chair Betsy Duke. "The leadership and insight that these directors brought to the board and its committees, including the board's Human Resources, Finance, Risk, and Corporate Responsibility committees are just some of the many ways they served our board with distinction over the years."[5] A very distinguished send-off, indeed. But where were these directors during the worst scams perpetuated by bankers in our lifetime? Perhaps, the Corporate Responsibility committee should have been re-named the Corporate Irresponsibility committee. No "refreshment" there, let alone a pause.

The name Wells Fargo is forever linked with the image of a six-horse stagecoach thundering across the American West, loaded with gold. From the Gold Rush to the early twentieth century, through prosperity, depression and war, Wells Fargo earned a reputation of trust due to its attention and loyalty to customers.[7] Where did it go wrong? Why? How did such a prestigious company lose its way? You'll find all the sordid details in the ensuing chapters.

In 1852, Henry Wells and William Fargo founded Wells, Fargo & Co. to serve the west and, after the completion of the transcontinental railroad in 1869, expanded to the Northeast into New York. Wells Fargo, having dropped the comma after Wells, became the country's first nationwide express company. It adopted the motto "Ocean to Ocean" to describe its service that connected over 2,500 communities in twenty-five states, and "Over-the-Seas" to highlight its lines linking America's increasingly global economy.

In 1905, Wells Fargo & Co.'s Bank San Francisco formerly separated from Wells Fargo & Co. Express also known as American Express. It survived the 1906 San Francisco earthquake and fire. Bank president I.W. Hellman telegraphed, "Building Destroyed, Vault Intact, Credit Unaffected."[8]

In the 1910s and 1920s, Wells Fargo served as a commercial bank in San Francisco, supporting the West's growing business and agriculture, including the fledgling auto, aerospace and film industries. The Wells Fargo Stagecoach became a regular in Hollywood westerns. Through the twentieth century, Wells Fargo expanded from just one office in San Francisco where it had a premier downtown location (next to the Sutro & Co. building in which I worked) to the entire west and beyond.

In the late 1990s, it was the country's ninth largest bank and, in 2015, the most valuable bank in the world, ahead of Industrial and Commercial Bank of China. As of June, 2017, it was No. 2 globally, behind only JPMorgan Chase. In 2018, it had 8,200 locations in forty-two countries and territories and 13,000 ATMs. With approximately

265,000 "team members", it has served one in three households in the U.S. It was ranked No. 25 on *Fortune*'s 2017 rankings of America's largest corporations. Now, one year later, look at it. A total disgrace. How and why did it happen?

Have you seen the new TV commercials? They read: *"Established in 1852. Re-established in 2018 with a recommitment to you."*

The TV advertising campaign was rolled out nationally on major network evening newscasts as well as on the Sunday talk shows. Wells Fargo was also buying ads on major Spanish language networks. The 2010 Annual Report, with its John Stumpf rallying cry, is giving it another try in the 2019 Annual Report with the name "Rebuilding Trust." We'll see if it is successful.

CHAPTER 3

WHAT? YOU DIDN'T OPEN UP THAT ACCOUNT?

"I don't want anyone ever offering a product to someone when they don't know what the benefit is, or the customer doesn't understand it, or doesn't want it, or doesn't need it."[1] Pray tell, who uttered these inspiring words? Hard to believe, but this was the big boast by the uninspiring leader of what was the third largest bank in the world, John Stumpf, chief executive of Wells Fargo Bank, in an interview with *The San Francisco Chronicle* in September, 2016. Gulp! These are hard words to swallow.

Nearly a year after Wells Fargo's fraudulent account scandal shocked the banking world, the bank said it had turned up more than a million additional accounts that customers may not have authorized. This brought the number to 3.5 million – a nearly 70% increase over the bank's initial estimate. Some customers learned about the accounts only when they were charged fees for them. Sadly, employees who met the bank's sales goals received bonuses and those who did not, risked losing their jobs. It was a case of "You win. I lose."

Not so fast. Former employees who said they were fired for following the law filed a class-action lawsuit seeking $2.6 billion or more in damages claiming they were fired for NOT making sales quotas. The suit alleged wrongful termination, unlawful business practices and failure to pay overtime among other things. The Office of the Comptroller of the Currency (OCC) had identified problems with Wells Fargo's sales practices as far back as 2010 but failed to take timely action to halt the abuses. An internal report by the OCC posted online in April, 2017, said it missed opportunities to launch an earlier and deeper investigation of approximately 700 whistle-blower complaints by employees. The report said there were multiple red flags and missed signals at the OCC for years.

So what was the result? It wasn't pretty. The OCC slapped a $1 billion penalty punishing the bank for abuses that harmed mortgage and auto loan borrowers, and for what regulators said was a pervasive and "reckless" lack of risk management practices because it failed to maintain a compliance risk program that was appropriate for a bank of its size and complexity. That failure, the OCC maintained, allowed the bank to "engage in reckless unsafe or unsound practices and violations of law."[2] President Trump tweeted that penalties against the bank could be "substantially increased."

"Outrageous" and "a major breach of trust"[3] is how local and federal regulators described Wells Fargo's behavior that pushed thousands of employees to open those fake accounts. The new fine dwarfed the previous massive $185 million settlement—$100 million to the CFPB, $50 million to the city and county of Los Angeles and $35 million to the OCC. The bank did not admit any wrongdoing but it apologized to customers and announced steps to change its sales practices. It set aside $5 million to cover refunds to customers.

Despite the refunds, some customers said it wouldn't be so easy to undo the damage. Jerry Van Vort, at the time a community college student, said he visited a Wells Fargo branch and was offered a new credit card. He turned down the offer, but weeks later he received one in the mail. He didn't close the account and later discovered that the credit card was linked to his checking account to provide overdraft protection. "I didn't have enough money in my checking account and the overdraft went into the credit card. I had to pay that off,"[4] he explained. He said he believed this damaged his credit history, making it more expensive to borrow money and harder for him to qualify for a mortgage.

In addition, U.S. District Judge Vince Chhabria approved a $142 million settlement. Calling it "rough justice,"[5] it would pay an average of $35 for those victimized account holders. "There's no doubt this is an imperfect solution, but what's the alternative?" he asked. "I do believe this settlement is fair and there was a conscientious effort by both parties to come up with the least-worse solution for what's happened here."[6]

Let's not forget the attorneys' fees. The law firm of Keller Rohrback L.L.P. or "KR" presented a detailed case to the court requesting a fee of $21,300,000, which was 15% of the $142 million class-action Settlement Fund. Case in point – an hourly rate of $710–$995 for partners, $400–$650 for associates, and $225–$325 for paralegals and professional staff.

Wells Fargo isn't the only bank where fake accounts were opened. A federal review in 2016, triggered by the bank's scandal found that "weaknesses" at other banks caused employees to open accounts without customer consent, according to the Comptroller of the Currency. A review of more than 40 large and midsize banks concluded that the cause of these bogus accounts included "short-term sales promotions without adequate risk controls," deficient procedures and other isolated instances of "employee misconduct."[7]

Besides the additional accounts that were revealed, a wider review uncovered a new issue: unauthorized enrollments in the bank's online bill payment service. Wells Fargo said it found an astonishing 528,000 cases in which customers may have signed up without their knowledge or consent. The bank said it would refund $910,000 to those customers who incurred fees or charges. The service is now free.

Senator Elizabeth Warren, chair of the Senate Banking Committee, unleashed a scathing statement saying: "Unbelievable. Wells Fargo's massive fraud is even worse than we thought."[8] A coalition of thirty-three consumer groups sent a letter to congressional leaders urging them to bring Wells Fargo executives back to Capitol Hill where former CEO John Stumpf appeared before unhappy lawmakers the year before.

Wells Fargo customers and former employees said they tried to alert bank executives of actions by branch managers as far back as 2005.

An investigation commissioned by the board found signs of abuses that occurred in 2002, but newly installed CEO Timothy Sloan said the bank could look back no earlier than 2009 because it did not have sufficient data on previous periods.

Besides opening the fake accounts, Wells Fargo had the audacity of closing accounts if criminal activity occurred in an account such as a counterfeit check or an unauthorized withdrawal. If such fraud does appear, a bank is required by law to investigate the matter. According to a former employee, the bank had a simpler solution – close the account and drop the customer.

Matthew Valles was employed in the banking industry at American Express. While there, he received regular promotions and raises. He left AMEX to work for Wells Fargo where he became a Financial Crimes Specialist in the Internet Service Group Online Fraud Operations, a position in which he investigated reports of online fraud pertaining to Wells Fargo's customer savings accounts, checking accounts, and credit accounts. After a year, he was promoted and personally helped uncover the now publicly known Wells Fargo scheme involving an internal fraud ring used by branch employees to create fake customer accounts.

As a result of his contributions and positive work record, he provided training to other Wells Fargo investigators and was given the opportunity to take on a higher position at his Salt Lake City office but turned down the offer to pursue a different opportunity at Wells Fargo's Portland office. He claimed he was told by his supervisors that the new position would give him broader knowledge of various types of fraud that would ultimately help him to be promoted to another position. Subsequently, he was hired and relocated to the Portland area. In this new job, he worked with investigators in Wells Fargo's Loss Prevention Line of Business Referrals unit to investigate internal fraud submitted by employees to a confidential internal database.

Almost immediately, upon starting in his new position, be became concerned about the internal culture of the unit. He claimed he soon discovered that the apparent directive of the unit – as indicated by Wells Fargo management – was to meet Wells Fargo metrics at all costs, even if it meant failing to adequately disclose instances of fraud in customer accounts. By failing to do this, the Loss Prevention Line of Business Referrals unfairly shifted losses caused by fraud to Wells Fargo's own customers, many of whom had been victims of identity theft and unauthorized withdrawals from their checking and savings accounts. Rather than conduct a thorough investigation into claims of fraud, he began to notice that the bank would instead save money by simply closing accounts under the pretext of "business decision to close."[9] Improperly closing accounts in this manner ensured that customers, not Wells Fargo, were left to absorb the costs. This decision also unfairly harmed customers' credit in cases where fraud had caused an account to be overdrawn.

In early 2015, Valles suffered a serious health event that caused him to be hospitalized and was approved for leave from April 24 to June 22, 2015 and for a few days in July. After his hospitalizations, his supervisor reportedly chastised and treated him worse than other employees, and refused to train him properly, apparently in retaliation for his requests for medical leave. Soon after returning to work, he complained to the human resources department about the bank's illegal failure to properly investigate reports of fraud and its illegal behavior in closing accounts. He also complained about illegal retaliation from his supervisor based on his hospitalization and leave. The unit to which he was assigned was later investigated, and his supervisor was transferred out of the unit. The supervisor who replaced him was reportedly hostile toward him and tried to isolate him from the work of the unit. She would not allow him to work remotely or to use a laptop and denied him opportunities for overtime and promotions.

Due to his serious health condition, he had to take a number of subsequent medical leaves and, each time he returned to work, he observed his supervisor became more hostile toward him. When he requested minor schedule changes in order to accommodate his medical conditions, she constantly refused. In one instance, she attempted to discipline him because he was cooperating too much with a law enforcement agent seeking information about fraud that took place in a customer's account. This convinced him that the unit was not committed to thoroughly investigate fraudulent activities in customer accounts. She retaliated against him by firing him. She lied and said he was terminated because he had committed another security violation by leaving his notebook on his desk, which contained an internal case number.

Valles was at a loss as to what his next job would be and feared that Wells Fargo's wrongful termination would limit his ability to get another similar position in the banking industry. In a filing dated August 4, 2017, Wells Fargo disclosed to the public that it was under investigation for the very account closure scheme Valles had internally blown the whistle about as alleged in his complaint. Wells Fargo's disclosure is below:

CONSUMER DEPOSIT ACCOUNT REGULATORY INVESTIGATION

> *The Consumer Financial Protection Bureau (CFPB) has commenced an investigation into whether customers were unduly harmed by the Company's procedures regarding the freezing (and, in many cases, closing) of consumer deposit accounts after the Company detected suspected fraudulent activity (by third-parties or account holders) that effected those accounts.*

In a lawsuit dated February 29, 2018, **MATTHEW VALLES,** Plaintiff, v. **WELLS FARGO BANK N.A.** and **KIMBERLY THRUSH,** Defendants, Mr. Valles respectfully requested:

A) An injunction stopping Wells Fargo from retaliating against any other employee in a manner similar to the retaliation alleged in this complaint;

B) A judgment against Wells Fargo holding it liable for retaliating against Mr. Valles as alleged in this complaint;

C) A judgment against Wells Fargo allowing actual damages up to $20 million plus interest and reimbursed fees, costs and expenses; and

D) Any other equitable relief this Court deems appropriate.

Mr. Valles intends to amend this complaint with leave of Court to add a claim for punitive damages up to $180 million and may intend to add additional defendants and claims as information is learned in discovery. Mr. Valles respectfully requests trial by jury.

Copies of this lawsuit were sent to various federal and state government officials, the Federal Reserve Board of Governors, Wells Fargo officials and to Wells Fargo's largest shareholder, Berkshire Hathaway c/o CEO Warren Buffett and Vice Chair Charles Munger.

Despite the ill feelings of his firing, Valles did say Wells Fargo had shown signs of progress: "They're working on fixing the problems. A lot needed to be done."[10] At an investor conference in 2018, Sloan said that the bank was reviewing its procedures for handling accounts with signs of suspicious activity. But, apparently, it took a lawsuit to move things forward.

However, any changes that are made will not help customers whose accounts have already been affected. Michael and Mary Ellen Mervis, who had accounts with Wells Fargo for decades, discovered that one of their accountants had removed a six-figure sum from their checking account without their consent over several years. They filed a police report and alerted the bank. Soon after, Wells Fargo told them that it was closing their checking and brokerage accounts and would not let them open new deposit accounts. When the Mervises protested, the bank responded by noting its "responsibilities to oversee and manage risk in banking operations,"[11] and said the decision was final. That forced them to find another bank and transfer their assets but still left them on their own to pursue their missing money. The accountant was eventually convicted of theft and ordered to make restitution, but they still hadn't received all their money as of February, 2018. Mr. Mervis said, "We got hold of a lady in the fraud department and she said this happened to a lot of people who filed fraud complaints. We were horrified. The bank had this attitude that if something went wrong, instead of trying to fix it, they were just going to run you over with the stagecoach and be done with you."[12]

Wells Fargo said that it had completed its investigation into unauthorized accounts and did not expect to uncover significantly more. "This is an important milestone to rebuild trust," Sloan said on a call with reporters. He called the discovery of additional unauthorized accounts "a reminder of the disappointment that we caused our customers."[13] The bank has made sweeping changes in the wake of the scandal, including overhauling its executive lineup, replacing key board members, revamping its internal controls and risk management, and emphasizing to its bank branch workers that it wants them to focus on customer service, not sales. No more "stores," just branches. And not a moment too soon.

CHAPTER 4

FROM THE KILLING FIELDS TO WELLS FARGO

He was not your typical whistleblower. In fact, he was not your typical American citizen. Duke Tran (born Tran Duy Duc) escaped from slavery and ultimately became a slave by working at Wells Fargo.

Tran was born in Vietnam in 1961, the son of a colonel in the South Vietnamese military fighting alongside American troops. He was thirteen when North Vietnam took over the government and sent his father to a prison camp as punishment for helping the Americans. When he was released four years later, his father paid to sneak him over the Cambodian border. His father told him, "You have to leave."[1]

But as soon as he was over the border, he was captured by fighters for the genocidal Khmer Rouge regime and forced to drink vinegar as his captors believed he had swallowed gold and family jewels that vinegar would help expel. At seventeen, he became a slave and was forced to dig wells. "Sometimes the soldiers got drunk and took me out and put AK-47s to my head so I would pass out, "[2] he remembered.

Eight months later, his captors traded him to aid workers who carried humanitarian supplies such as a kilo of rice, two boxes of canned tuna, two boxes of sardines in tomato sauce, antibiotics and some other medical supplies. The aid workers took him to Thailand and from there, the International Organization for Migration helped him get to the United States. "I am so grateful. Here I am, an American citizen."[3]

His first job was scrubbing pots in a restaurant. Soon after that, he got his first call center job in the payment processing division of a local bank. He worked in call centers for twenty-five years. But nothing prepared him for his job at the Wells Fargo home equity division.

He was proud of his work and described himself as "a really model employee" who was recognized for his good work. The division was responsible for a portfolio of loans that Wells Fargo purchased from another company at the peak of the financial crisis. After examining the loans, employees realized that the bank was missing some of the paperwork that proved the borrowers owed the bank money. A Wells Fargo spokesman confirmed the problem and said 120 of the loans initially appeared to be missing their underlying documents.

After nine months, Tran answered a phone call from an eighty-eight-year-old customer who had opened up a letter that Wells Fargo sent to his wife. He handled her affairs because she had Alzheimer's. The letter said that she owed the bank around $90,000 and that if she didn't pay within ninety days, the bank would foreclose on their house. She did have credit card accounts but this was the first he had heard of any loan. "I knew that she had taken out a mortgage," he said but "my house was paid off thirty-five years ago."[4] He then called the bank and spoke to Tran. He asked him for proof that his wife owed the money. Tran tried to pull up the file on his computer, but he couldn't find the loan documents. He said they were missing.

Tran started calling various Wells Fargo offices to figure out what had happened and consulted bank archives to find the documents, but they were unsuccessful. Tran talked to his boss and was told not to follow up. They tell me: It's no problem. If the customer calls back, you tell them it's a "balloon" payment referring to a type of loan that would require the customer to repay the amount owed all at once. He wasn't the only employee to receive that advice.

Tran charged in a lawsuit against Wells Fargo that he felt uncomfortable as soon as he saw how the customer's inquiry was handled. In Tran's view, the customer was demanding proof that any loan had existed at all and said he had shared his feelings with his boss. Soon afterward, he received another unsettling phone call. This time, it was from a woman who said the bank had told her that she owed $165,000. She, too, said she had not taken out a loan and was really emotional. "I have all my children live in my home. I don't have any money to pay. Where is my children going to live?"[5] Once again, the bank had no paperwork to prove that she owed the money. Tran complained to his supervisor and his boss's boss. "I told them this is a fraud; I cannot be part of that."[6]

Another customer complained he started receiving letters from Wells Fargo Recovery about his student loan. He had been making regular payments and said they continuously switch their collection reps around so he gets a new letter every 3-6 months. Each time he gets a new rep, they attempt to settle for 50%. He said he could probably do that but chose to continue to send them $300 a month. He still owed around $6000. The week before, he received a call from the latest rep. She was demanding $1,600 plus $350 per month or they would take him to court.

Another customer said he had closed a savings account but kept a checking and credit card accounts open but was not using them. He still managed to accrue debt somehow. So he called the debit and credit departments and cancelled those accounts. When he did, he asked, "Are these accounts paid off? I do not have any debts or balances to pay after closing?" and they said no (or I would have paid it). Subsequently, he got two letters from "IC System" (collections) saying his accounts with Wells Fargo are past due. "We have been asked by WFB to begin debt collection activity over less than $45 but more than $35." He called the WF past due telephone number and was put on hold for forty-five minutes before he realized it may be smarter to ask if there was a better way to get this debt cancelled. So he left a message; "Should I just pay the money to prevent it from hitting my credit report or how should I go about freezing this? Thanks!" No response.

In a court filing, Tran's supervisor said: "I had no knowledge that Mr. Tran reported or complained of what he believed to be an alleged Wells Fargo practice of deceiving customers regarding missing loan documents or other unlawful activities."[7] Afterward, his boss called him into his office where a group of his superiors was waiting. They asked for his security badge and told him he was fired. His boss and a Wells lawyer escorted him out the front door. Tran recalled: "I'm thinking I'm going to die. From the time they walk me out that door, I don't have any backup."[8] He was told if he had any questions about why he was fired, he could call a H.R. representative. When he did call, he was told he had been fired for failing to orally respond to a customer whose call he had answered. Tran was mortified. He couldn't sleep and couldn't tell his wife and their two sons that he had been fired. When they asked him why he wasn't going to work in the mornings, he told them he was on vacation. "I thought, my God, I've lost my American dream."[9] His wife worked in a factory paying $17 per hour and suddenly it became the family's only income.

After being without a job for three months, he got a call center job at US Bank. But he still was angry about what he thought was an unfair firing. He subsequently sued Wells Fargo for retaliation and other claims. His lawyers argued that Wells tried to silence him and, when that didn't work, he was fired. Tran wanted to go to trial but his lawyers wanted a jury to award him for damages and compensation. What Tran really wanted was to force Wells Fargo to publicly admit its shady practices. The company's lawyers maintained that the bank fired him for poor performance and that he never reported anything to his superiors. Tran's trial lawyer said he could not foresee Tran's settling for less than $10 million. But Tran did not want to settle. Instead, he just wanted Wells to admit what it did was wrong. "They have so much money. They use that money to buy off the American justice system, and they never go to court. I'm ready to go to court. I'm not going to settle."[10] But the next day, he did settle. As for the customer who protested that the bank had spent three years trying to collect money he never borrowed, when he was told the size of the settlement, a reported seven figures, he laughed: "That's good for him. He hasn't anything to worry about now."[11] As for he and his wife who were still battling the bank, he said, "I think we should be compensated for the trouble they've caused us."[12]

CHAPTER 5

"LIKE LIONS HUNTING ZEBRAS"

That's how a former Wells Fargo banker described the abuses put on by the bank against Mexican immigrants who speak little English, older persons with memory problems and small-business owners with several lines of credit.

Kevin Pham, a former Wells Fargo employee in San Jose, California, which has a high Mexican population, described the disgraceful behavior that happened far too often at the branch where he worked: "They would look for the weakest, the ones that would put up the least resistance. The analogy I use was that it was 'like lions hunting zebras.'"[1] The absence of a Social Security number made it easier for Wells Fargo employees to open fraudulent accounts in those customers' names. Coincidentally, the bank is one of the few major banks to permit accounts to be opened without Social Security numbers. Pham put it this way: "Bankers wanted the quickest, easiest sale – the low-hanging fruit. The extreme pressure forced people into it."[2]

At a branch in Scottsdale, Arizona, members of a local Native American community would arrive like clockwork every three months with checks for their share of the community's casino revenue. Ricky M. Hansen, Jr., a former branch manager there, said that some bankers would try to dupe them into opening unnecessary accounts laden with fees.

He learned that one branch manager had invented "per capita day packages," which included five or more bank accounts. Customers were told that they needed separate accounts for such purposes as traveling, grocery shopping and savings for an emergency.

"They would deposit their money and get hit with fees like crazy, because they got confused about what account they were using," Hansen said. "They would use the wrong debit card and overdraw their travel account, and then when they came back three months later, they would lose hundreds of dollars from their next check paying off those fees."[3]

In Illinois, one former teller described watching in frustration as older customers became victims of the Wells Fargo ploy. Brandi Baker, who worked at a branch in Galesburg, said, "We had customers of all ages, but the elderly ones would at times be targeted because they don't ask many questions about fees and such."[4]

In the Los Angeles area, college campuses were considered prime spots for employees seeking to open up new accounts because younger customers had a tendency to trust a banker's advice and who would question what's told to them by a bank representative?

"So the customer essentially handed the banker a blank check," said Athena McDaniel-Watkins, a former employee. "The banker was then able to list as many accounts under that application as he wanted or, in many cases, as many as he needed to hit sales goals for that day."[5]

Steven Curtis, who also worked at several Wells Fargo branches in the L.A. area, said that when college students showed up asking for overdraft fees to be waived, bankers would sometimes tell them they could do so only by closing their account and opening a batch of new ones. The practices in California were also described in a lawsuit the Los Angeles city attorney filed against Wells Fargo in 2015. Among the complaints was that employees specifically sought out Mexican citizens because their identity documents were easier to misuse. If customers complained, employees advised them "to ignore the unauthorized fees and letters from collection agencies because the lack of a Social Security number means the debt will not affect them."[6]

Ashlie Storms, a former banker at a branch in West Milford, N.J., said she quit her job soon after learning that a banker at another branch manipulated the accounts of one of Ms. Storms' regular customers, an older woman with memory problems. She had come to deposit a large check, only to have the banker use it to open new checking and savings accounts without her approval. The next day, she and her daughters went to the branch, confused about where her money had gone and why she couldn't gain access to it. "What should have been a five-minute conversation turned into a three-hour complaint to corporate about the actions this banker decided to take without the customer's consent," Ms. Storms said. "The banker was a top producer for our region, always receiving recognition from management for her sales."[7] That should have waved a red flag as top producers in many companies that "handle" clients' money are not all trustworthy. But Wells Fargo apparently was overjoyed with the results and looked the other way and tacitly jumped for joy. I saw this behavior in the stock brokerage business over many years and was appalled. Greed got you to the top in one major firm at which I worked and I couldn't wait to leave.

A group that coalesced on Facebook declared November 12 "National Close Your Wells Fargo Account Day." Some people weren't waiting until then. Michael Masterson posted on the group's Facebook page about refinancing his mortgage to move it away from Wells Fargo. "This was an action I took as an individual looking to sever ties with what I regard as a dishonest financial institution,"[8] he emailed.

When CEO Stumpf testified before members of Congress—once in the Senate and once in the House—he was pressed hard on whether any demographic group had been disproportionately affected. He said he was not sure. Of the two million potentially unauthorized accounts the bank uncovered in its internal review, the affected customers "skewed to younger people, not older people,"[9] he told the House Financial Services Committee.

After the Senate Banking Committee held its hearing, it followed up with a letter containing fifty-eight additional questions for the bank because Stumpf had since left the bank. Among them: "What proportion of the harmed customers are old, members of ethnic minorities or military veterans?" As of October, 2016, the committee was still waiting for a response.

In October, 2017, Wells Fargo was ordered to return $3.4 million to customers after selling them inappropriate investment products. From July 2010 to May 2012, FINRA (the Financial Industry Regulatory Authority) charged that Wells Fargo brokers sold risky exchange-traded products (ETPs) to at least 1,300 who had moderate and conservative risk profiles. The bank also failed to make sure brokers unloaded these products from the accounts within thirty days. The payments ranged from under $1 to $80,000, with many totaling several hundred or a few thousand dollars.

The products' value shifted based on market volatility over short durations, but some brokers mistakenly believed they could be used as long-term hedges against a market downturn, FINRA said. Although Wells Fargo had procedures in place to ensure the products were sold only under certain circumstances, FINRA said the bank failed to implement them correctly or have a "reasonable system" to supervise how and when those securities were sold and did not properly train brokers. In doing so, the bank violated two securities rules.

The securities in question were appropriate only for short-term investors and were likely to lose significant value over time. As an example, the risk posed by one of the most popular choices lost 99.97% of its value since its inception in 2009. "It is absolutely evil," said Joe Saluzzi, an expert on market structure, co-head of trading at Themis Trading and co-author of the book "Broken Markets." "Obviously, Wells Fargo had no idea what they were selling. It's not meant for retail. Everyone gets trapped in it."[10] Morningstar researcher Adam McCullough warned that holding on to volatility-linked products has "cost investors dearly over the long run."[11]

Phil Aidikoff, a securities lawyer in Los Angeles who represents investors and brokers, said cases like this involving investment products are common. Brokers at big firms, he said, typically don't analyze investment products themselves and instead rely on their firms to perform due diligence. If the company says a product isn't too risky for ordinary investors, brokers will offer it, even if they don't understand it. "You have some brokers who have been in the business a long time, and you have some guys who were selling stereo equipment six months ago. If brokers understood what the investment was, they shouldn't have sold it. But they didn't understand. They simply relied on what they were told by the company."[12]

CHAPTER 6

WANTED CAR INSURANCE? NEEDED HOME INSURANCE? WELLS FARGO TOOK YOU FOR A RIDE

Wells Fargo charged as many as 570,000 customers for car insurance they didn't need and about 20,000 of those customers may have defaulted on their car loans and had their vehicles repossessed in part because of these unnecessary insurance costs. The number of customers hurt by this may have been even larger than the bank admitted. An internal report prepared by a consulting firm and obtained by *The New York Times* found that more than 800,000 customers were affected, including 25,000 who had their cars repossessed. Active-duty service members were also caught up in the scandal. Wells Fargo was accused by the government of illegally repossessing 413 cars owned by service members without a court order.

Officials of the Federal Reserve Bank of San Francisco where the bank is headquartered had inquired into a different, specialized type of insurance that is sold to customers when they buy a car. This is not the same insurance purchased by borrowers on car loans. This is called guaranteed auto protection insurance or GAP, which is intended to protect a lender against the fact that a car—the collateral for its loan—loses significant value the moment it is driven off the lot. It costs between $400 to $600. There are car dealers who push it, and lenders like it because of the protection it provides. But when borrowers pay off the loan early, they are entitled to a refund of some of the premium because the coverage is no longer needed. It was reported that Wells Fargo never paid the refunds.

Subsequently, Wells Fargo did promise to pay $64 million in cash refunds on top of $16 million in account adjustments. That works out to an average of just $140 for each of the 570,000 customers impacted. The bank said it would work with credit bureaus to correct errors in customers' credit records. The bank may have also failed to properly notify customers about the additional insurance charges in Arkansas, Michigan, Mississippi, Tennessee and Washington, which have tougher disclosure requirements. Those 60,000 customers were to get about $39 million. Wells Fargo blamed the problem on "inadequate" checks and balances at the bank as well as flaws in the systems of the company that handled the insurance policies. In a statement, the bank's head of consumer lending, Franklin Codel, said, "We take full responsibility for our failure."[1] New York City Comptroller Scott Stringer said, "This is a full-blown scandal—again. It's unbelievable, outrageous, sad and yet quintessential Wells Fargo."[2] Stringer manages the city's pension funds, which held about $11.5 million Wells Fargo shares as of April, 2017.

The biggest shareholder was Warren Buffett's Berkshire Hathaway, which owned 473 million shares or a 9.92% stake as of May, 2017. Buffett was anything but a happy camper. He said they had yet to completely "remove the stain," referring to those that performed or condoned those scandalous acts. "What you find is there's never just one cockroach in the kitchen when you start looking around," Berkshire Hathaway's chairman and CEO said on Squawk Alley.[3]

"Anytime you put focus on an organization that has hundreds of thousands of people, you may very well find that it wasn't just one who misbehaved that you find out about." he said. "It's a terrific bank. There were some things that were done very wrong there but they are being corrected." Buffett, known as "The Oracle of Omaha," said that Wells Fargo seemed to be blinded by the fact that the banking industry had gotten used to paying billions of dollars in fines for mortgage malpractices and $185 million seemed paltry by comparison, referring to the fine Wells Fargo was fined for opening up unauthorized accounts.

"They measured the seriousness of the problem by the dimensions of the fine and they thought it signaled a less-offensive practice." Asked if he thought all of the problems had been exposed, Buffett replied, "I think so, but that's what you never know," he said in February, 2018. "My guess is, and it's just a guess, is that they have scrubbed and scrubbed and found out the things that were done wrong but the regulators would make them pay...for past sins. As much as possible you want the people responsible to pay." He suggested in 2011 that directors should have five years of their pay clawed back.

At Berkshire's annual meeting that year, he declared: "The CEO and spouse should be put at risk of growing broke. This is especially true of the CEO, but the board should suffer huge penalties as well. Perhaps they should have to repay the last **five years** of director's fees. If you run a firm that needs to be saved, then the person running that institution should be aware that it is very painful to fail."

Following were the payments to directors in 2016:

Cash Retainer	$75,000
Stock Component	$180,000
Independent chairman retainer	$250,000
Independent vice chairman retainer	$100,000
Committee chair fees	$25,000–$40,000
Regular or special board or committee meeting fee	$2,000

At the meeting, he lashed out at what was going on before their eyes: "They totally underestimated the impact of what they had done once it became uncovered. It was a huge, huge, huge error if the company received internal calls from employees flagging misbehavior and decided to ignore them. The main problem was that they didn't act when they learned about it."[4] Buffett also harshly criticized the bank's incentive system noting that workers were paid, graded and promoted based on the number of services they sold to customers. "It turned out that it incentivized the wrong kind of behavior."[5]

As for Tim Sloan, as of October, 2016, he still had Buffett's confidence but his thirty-year tenure at Wells Fargo may well have put him in disrepute with other shareholders and the board of directors. In his testimony before the Senate Banking Committee, he repeatedly admitted that the actions taken to fix the bank's sales practices when they first became known in 2013 were insufficient and not aggressive enough at a time when he was Chief Financial Officer. In a 2018 interview with CNBC, Buffett said he had confidence in Sloan who he said had been "working like crazy"[6] to resolve the mess.

Meanwhile, *Dealbreaker* reported that Sloan replacing Stumpf was not exactly reassuring. According to his bio, Sloan had been at Wells Fargo longer than Stumpf and was Carrie Tolstedt's boss and according to *Reuters*, "he had oversight over Wells' retail division which cranked out those millions of fake accounts, some of them during his tenure as COO." Thornton McEnery wrote at *Dealbreaker*: Promoting a guy that had arguably closer ties to unauthorized accounts, and then acting like it's a symbol of institutional change, is the kind of thing that makes Elizabeth Warren salivate with righteous rage."[7] Khalid Taha, a former Wells Fargo personal banker who left and sued over sales pressures, told *Reuters*: "Wells Fargo's problems go from top to bottom. Sloan is part of the problem. I can't see him as a solution."[8]

Elizabeth Warren didn't mince words at the Senate's Banking Committee hearing. She told Sloan he was at best "incompetent" and at worst, "complicit," and "either way, you should be fired. Wells Fargo is not going to change with you in charge."[9] She noted that Sloan was one of the executives "leading Wells Fargo during the time of a years-long scam."[10]

Senator John Neely Kennedy directed his attack against Sloan by asking, "What in god's name were you thinking? I'm not against large; I'm happy when businesses are successful. I'm not against big. With all due respect, I'm against dumb."[11] Senator Sherrod Brown asked, "Why should we believe you're committed to changing your bank's practices and being fair to customers when you continue to use that behind-closed-doors arbitration system that clearly doesn't allow customers their day in court?"[12]

Like some other former employees who complained that the bank had continued to push the sales goals, Taha said, "We were warned about this type of behavior but the reality was that people had to meet their goals. They needed a paycheck."[13] Someone else who also needed a job was Yesemia Guitron, the sole provider of her two children. "The economy had shut down," she recalled. She was hired as a personal banker and soon had heard negative things about the environment at Wells, but she didn't have many options. "I needed the job." Soon after she was hired, "I realized why all the other bankers had left."

In a lawsuit she later filed, customers were coming to her, complaining about getting mail from Wells Fargo on accounts or services that they never authorized. "People knew me and knew I could fix the problem."[14] Most of the customers were Spanish-speaking, like her, so they didn't feel comfortable going to management in English. "All the tellers and staff knew it, but no one else would complain," she said. "People needed the job. So did I, but I knew right from wrong." In an email she sent to her branch manager, she wrote: "I have come across instances where I've opened up accounts and shortly after they are closed and new sets of accounts are opened. I find NO banker notes to explain why this is happening. I am very concerned as I know this to be GAMING!!!"[15] She collected approximately 300 printouts of accounts that were problematic in various ways such as a minor having more than a dozen accounts. When she raised concerns on more than one hundred occasions, her manager began to retaliate, making it harder for her to meet her sales goals, and she was subsequently fired.

"The branch managers were always asking, 'How many solutions did you sell today?'" said Sharif Kellogg, a former employee. "They wanted three to four a day. In my mind, that was crazy—that's not how people's financial lives work." He said he was constantly being hounded by his supervisor to increase his sales, or "solutions," as they were known. "I was always getting written up for failing to bump my solutions numbers up." [16]

Julie Tishkoff, an administrative assistant to a Wells Fargo regional president, said, according to her discrimination complaint, she observed "fraudulent banking practices," including employees "forging customer signatures and opening accounts for customers without their knowledge or consent"[17] and soliciting elderly or other vulnerable customers to take out a line of credit even though they didn't understand the product.

Calling his brief stint at Wells "the lowest point in my life," Ken Mac, a fluent Chinese speaker, said he got an elderly Chinese woman to sign up for a credit card she didn't want by telling her "it was confirmation that she stopped by to update her address. I felt sick in my stomach," he said, "but it was a tough economy, and I was worried; if I lost my job, I would be in tough financial situation."[18]

One employee wrote to Stumpf's office in 2013: "I was in the 1991 Gulf War. I had less stress there than working for Wells Fargo." Others said they were warned that if they did not achieve sales goals, they would be transferred to a store where someone had been shot and killed or forced to walk out in the hot sun around the block.

Dennis Hambek, who moved from loan officer to branch manager complained: "We had a lot of longtime customers and a good staff, but the sales pressure kept mounting, mounting, mounting. Every morning, we had a conference call with all the managers. You were supposed to tell them how you were going to make your sales goal for the day, and if you didn't, you'd have to call in the afternoon to explain why you didn't make it and how you were going to fix it. It was really tense."[19] According to the Wells Fargo Code of Ethics, "Gaming" was defined as "the manipulation and/or misrepresentation of sales or referrals... in an attempt to receive compensation or to meet sales goals."[20] Hambeck recalled it was supposed to be a big no-no, so he called the Wells Fargo Ethics Line, and told his supervisor what he found. "This is blatant gaming but nobody seemed to care."[21] After his career, which spanned thirty-five years, he retired to avoid being fired for lack of productivity.

So, while the debate continued as to whether Sloan could accomplish the magic of cleaning things up, it wasn't a rabbit that came out of the hat, but a rat. Besides the car insurance scandal, Wells Fargo had come up with yet another one and this one was apparently much bigger than the monthly fees it charged for products like pet insurance to legal services that customers did not fully understand or necessarily want.

It was more like a nightmare instead of an American dream when Victor Muniz bought his first home, getting his mortgage through Wells Fargo. A lawsuit alleged Muniz was among many customers victimized by the bank's system that gouged home borrowers with improper fees to complete the mortgage process. Muniz sued the bank on interest- rate-locks of up to 90 days that Wells Fargo typically offered while mortgage applications are processed. If missing paperwork or other borrower-caused issues delay the closing beyond the specified time period, the borrower is charged a fee to extend the time. If the bank caused the delay, it is expected to forgo the fee. As an example, for a $200,000 mortgage, that amount could be $250. Muniz's lawsuit charged that Wells Fargo agreed to lock in a 5.875% interest rate on a 30-year fixed rate during the closing process. Nonetheless, he was charged $287.50 to extend the rate lock period when the mortgage processing bogged down amid "bank-caused delays."[22] Muniz had no choice but to accept the fee to timely complete the closing or he risked losing the home. He had already spent hundreds of dollars in closing-related costs such as the home inspection.

In a review by USA TODAY of complaints filed with a consumer agency, it found Wells Fargo customers in at least nine states raised similar concerns about mortgage fees. The bank said it would pay $108 million to the federal government to settle an investigation that claimed it charged veterans illegal fees to refinance their mortgages, costing taxpayers when those government-guaranteed mortgages defaulted.

Frank Chavez, a former Wells Fargo private mortgage banking employee, wrote a letter to Democratic members of the House Committee on Financial Services. He alleged that new financial regulations and Wells Fargo's processing changes and employee firings from 2012 through 2015 caused "a gradually increasing standstill and backlog of mortgage loan applications within the underwriting and loan closing process." Although some delays were caused by borrowers, the bank was responsible for "the vast majority of delays," the letter said. Trying to avoid having to absorb extra costs caused by such delays, the bank "systematically and wrongly"[23] shifted the blame to borrowers, forcing customers to pay fees.

A 2017 lawsuit filed by Mauricio Alaniz, a former mortgage consultant, alleged he told bank managers that paperwork for some of his customers was falsified by a Wells Fargo mortgage processor to make it appear that the borrowers were responsible for delays that were actually the bank's fault.

Borrowers across the country made similar allegations. *USA TODAY*'s review of the Consumer Financial Protection Bureau found:

- A Michigan customer complained that the bank's extension fees "coincidentally happen to coincide with time sensitive occurrences such as [home] appraisals… thus resulting in the consumer being pressured to agree to the rate locks or risk starting the loan process all over again,"[24]
- A New Jersey mortgage borrower said the ban promised to waive rate lock extension fees but imposed a $3,800 charge just before closing." I could either go to closing or they would have to cancel the entire deal,"[25] the borrower wrote.
- An Oregon customer complained that "I felt forced in the last

minute to pay a rate lock extension of $810 because the appraiser selected by the bank (Wells Fargo) took almost two months to provide the appraisal,"[26]

- After many bank-caused delays, a Virginia borrower complained that "we now have a letter from them with over $7,000 in rate lock extension fees and still no anticipated settlement date."[27]

Patricia McCoy, a former official with the Consumer Financial Protection Bureau, said the disclosure about the mortgage rate fees fits a pattern. "Wells Fargo had a business model, until all of this came to light, that emphasized generating fees charged to consumers under duplicitous circumstances simply for the sake of padding revenue."[28]

According to former Wells Fargo employees, mortgages were routinely bogged down in paperwork delays and, when that occurred, supervisors instructed loan officers to blame and charge customers, even when the problems were the bank's fault. The practice was particularly common in the Oregon and Los Angeles County regions. One branch officer estimated that in 2015 and 2016, he oversaw 350 mortgages that needed rate lock extensions. He said the bank only paid the fee twice. But an internal review determined that the mortgage rate lock policy was, at times, not consistently applied. In some cases, borrowers were charged fees even though Wells Fargo was primarily responsible for the delays.

As of October, 2017, a total of about $98 million in rate lock extension fees were charged to 110,000 borrowers. Wells Fargo said it believed a "substantial number" of the charges were appropriate. It said it would contact them all between September, 2013 and February, 2017 and promised to give refunds to customers "who believe that shouldn't have paid those fees." Tim Sloan said the bank is paying the refunds "as part of our ongoing efforts to rebuild trust"[29] with customers.

And still another lawsuit alleged that Wells Fargo's merchant services division overcharged small businesses for processing credit card transactions. Business owners who tried to leave the bank were charged "massive early termination fees."[30] The "overbilling scheme" targeted less sophisticated businesses by using "deceptive language" in a 63-page contract designed to confuse them.[31] A former employee told *CNNMoney* that he was instructed to target these small businesses. "We used to be told to go out and club the baby seals, mom-and-pop-shops that had no legal support."[32] When he worked there from 2011 to 2013, it was nearly impossible for business owners to leave the merchant agreement. "God would have had a hard time. It really was like a shady used car deal."[33]

One of the businesses claimed it was assessed a $500 early termination fee after trying to leave. That was despite the fact that Wells Fargo claimed the contract stated there would be no such fee. Another claimed it was "pounded by excessive fees."[34] Even when it went out of business, the owner was told he still had to pay the fees because of a three-year term of which he wasn't aware. The bank eventually closed the account without a fee.

Apparently frustrated by federal banking authorities to finally straighten out its mess, Wells took action against about three dozen district managers for oversight failures and fired them all. The firings were the first to focus on district managers in the bank's efforts to address alleged improper sales practices after it settled with regulators in September 2016.

Also fired were two employees in its community lending and investment division in relation to a federal investigation into the bank's negotiation and procurement of low-income housing tax credits (LIHTCs) according to a report by Bloomberg. The two executives had been previously suspended. The Department of Justice looked into whether the bank colluded with developers to submit lowball bids on tax credits for low-income housing projects. Banks are the biggest buyers of tax credits because they get both a tax write-off and credit under the Community Reinvestment Act.

The firings didn't stop there. In August, 2018, Wells fired or suspended more than a dozen employees in its investment bank and was investigating dozens of others over alleged violations of the company's expense policy regarding after-hours meals. The issue centered on whether employees ranging from analysts to managing directors doctored receipts on dinners that they charged.[35] Wells Fargo, like other big banks, reimburses staffers for food that they order when they have to stay late at the office to work on deals and other assignments for clients. Some employees allegedly altered the time stamps on emailed receipts to make their meals eligible for reimbursement. The investigation started with relatively junior analysts and associates in the investment bank's San Francisco office and spread to New York and Charlotte, North Carolina.

Big banks that are members of the Federal Reserve System are chartered in the federal level. In 2003, California actually tried to revoke Wells Fargo's licenses for mortgage lending due to a dispute over charging excessive interest. But the bank argued that federal law trumped state law, and they could not be kicked out of any state due to that federal charter. In 2005, a federal appeals court agreed.

Wells Fargo and the agency that grants federal bank charters, the Office of the Comptroller of the Currency (OCC), should have to defend the position why banks deserve the right to open fake accounts, screw mortgage and auto-loan customers and close accounts in which fraud is detected but not investigated. The Wells Fargo case might just be the one hideous example of how the OCC grants charters and what should be done to force those who rip off customers to go out of business.

CHAPTER 7

A PEEK INSIDE WEALTH MANAGEMENT
DON'T LOOK TOO LONG

Wealth Management at Wells Fargo is actually the business of Wells Fargo Advisors, the ninth largest brokerage firm in the U.S. as of August, 2017, with $490 billion under management for retail clients. The subsidiary was formerly known as Wachovia Securities until May 1, 2009, when it legally changed names following Wells Fargo's acquisition of Wachovia Corporation. Wells traces its history to 1879, where it grew through mergers with many of the brokerage industry's regional and national firms. These included Wachovia Securities, A.G. Edwards, and Bache & Co. As of September, 2017, there were 15,000 Advisors.

Another day, another dollar made or lost. But those dollars didn't have to be lost if a Wells Fargo Advisor had put one of his clients with a substantial portfolio in the right product. The Advisor put the blame on the 2008 market crash. My retort was that nothing would have been lost if the Advisor would have been more concerned about the client's money instead of his commissions. It's called the Fiduciary Standard whereby the client's interest should always come first and not the commissions. This debate has been going on for years and the number of hearings with the SEC and broker groups has continued ad nauseum.

In 2009, the state of California accused Wells Fargo of fraud for the company's role in an investment meltdown that has been compared to the Bernard Madoff's Ponzi scheme. Attorney General Jerry Brown sued three Wells Fargo subsidiaries, alleging they committed securities fraud by telling California investors that $1.5 billion of risky securities sold to them "were

.e could get their money back in eight days. Now, it turns
ɔt like cash and people can't get their money back even
.ny months, and they're mad as hell."[1] The lawsuit sought
.e money invested by about 2,400 Californians in what are
.ction-rate securities marketed by the Wells Fargo subsidiaries.

ɔn-rate securities, generally backed by student loans, munic-
ipal bonds or other debt, have interest rates that are reset periodically
through auctions – sometimes as often as once a week. More than $330
billion were sold to investors attracted to their yields.

When the market for these securities collapsed in 2008, many investors couldn't sell them or if so, at a loss. Harry Newton, a private
investor who operates the AuctionRatePreferreds.org website, described these securities as "the largest fraud ever perpetuated by Wall
Street on investors. It dwarfs all frauds in history, including Madoff."[2]

Several financial service companies that issued them agreed to repurchase billions of dollars of the devalued securities to settle claims
by regulators that they defrauded investors. Wells Fargo's Wachovia
Corp. agreed to repurchase $1.5 billion from California investors in a
settlement with the state Department of Corporations.

Brown's lawsuit named Wells Fargo Investments, Wells Fargo Brokerage Services and Wells Fargo Institutional Services as defendants. It
alleged they began selling them in 2001 and continued to sell them right
up to the collapse of the market in 2008, despite signs that the market
was beginning to falter in the second half of 2007. The state alleged that
Wells Fargo sales personnel weren't properly trained in the auction-rate
securities market and that the risks weren't explained to clients, who included retirees and small businesses, the accounts ranging from $25,000
to the millions of dollars. In one case cited by Brown, a Bay Area company shifted $400,000 in working capital from a money market account
to auction-rate securities. The business intended to use the money to
expand but when the auction-rate market failed, the company couldn't
access the money and instead was forced to lay off workers.

Wells Fargo disputed the state's allegations and said it had taken steps to help customers affected by the collapse of the auction-rate market, including offering loans to tide them over. Andrew Stoltmann, an attorney representing several auction-rate securities investors with claims against brokerage firms, said it was "unfortunate that it's taken as long as it has for the California attorney general to act on the issue, but better late than never."[3] A spokesman for Brown countered: "We try to be careful in doing our work and bringing the strongest possible case."[4]

In 2017, federal regulators charged the bank sold dangerous investments it didn't understand. Wells Fargo was ordered to pay back $3.4 million to customers because advisors recommended products that were "highly likely to lose value over time."[5]

Wells Fargo did not admit or deny the charges. It did admit, however, the callous disregard for protocol by a Wells Fargo executive who used a luxurious Malibu mansion for her own benefit. The repossessed $12 million beach house was lost by victims of the Bernard Madoff fraud because they were unable to service their loans on the property. But after the bank took ownership, nearby residents became suspicious about activity there complaining that a family appeared to be using the house for long weekends, one in particular when about twenty people were ferried by dinghy from an offshore yacht to join in. Meanwhile, a local real estate agent told *The Los Angeles Times* that Wells Fargo was refusing to show the house to potential buyers. In responses to questions from the paper, Wells Fargo said its agreement with the prior owner required it to keep the home off the market "for a period of time" but declined to elaborate.

Philip Roman, an eighteen-year resident who lives a few homes away from the property, said "It's outrageous to take over a property like that, not make it available and then put someone from the bank in it."[6] Wells Fargo said its ethics code wouldn't allow employees to make personal use of the property that had been surrendered to satisfy debts. W Michael Hoffman, executive director for the Center for Business Ethics at Bentley University said, "For a business to allow this to happen in today's ethically charged climate is quite suicidal. And because Madoff's fraud was the root cause of the situation, it's like rubbing salt into the wounds of a national tragedy."[7] Wells Fargo issued a statement saying "a single team member" had been responsible for violating company policies and, "as a result, employment of this individual has been terminated. We deeply regret the activities that have taken place as they do not reflect the conduct we expect of our team members."[8]

In reviewing some of the Wells Fargo cases on FINRA Broker Check, this is what I discovered:

In a Houston, Texas office, a client stated that he advised the Financial Advisor that he did not wish to pay commissions in his fee-based account. Client stated that he paid commissions following the transfer of his account to the Financial Advisor. Damages were unspecified but estimated to exceed $5,000. The Advisor commented that the matter was closed as client failed to respond to a settlement offer.

In another case, client alleged that she should not have been invested in Enron because she is a conservative investor and Enron was speculative. Damages were estimated to exceed $5,000.

The Financial Advisor adamantly denied that the investment was not suitable and believed that it was consistent with the conservative account objectives. When the Enron Preferred was bought for the client it was rated "investment grade" by Moody's and S&P and suitable for a conservative investor. As things began to deteriorate at Enron, the Advisor spoke with the client the day before she was to leave on an overseas vacation. He said he told her that if she could not afford to take a loss of her investment in Enron Preferred, she should sell it. She chose to hold the Enron Preferred. Enron deteriorated further and the Enron Preferred dropped quite drastically. Although the client says she is conservative and has low risk tolerance, she chose to hold the Preferred once the credit rating had been dropped and after she was warned of a possible total loss of capital. This Financial Advisor was licensed in 34 states which made it almost impossible to adhere to the "Know Your Client" rule of FINRA (Financial Invest-ment Regulatory Authority).

In another case, client alleged the advisory fees charged were at a higher rate than what was promised from 2012–2018.

- Advisor was licensed in 19 states. This is highly unusual because advisors should meet with their clients prior to making suitable recommendations. This Advisor took and passed the Series 31 – Futures Managed Funds Exam. It appears to me that she was selling futures over the phone which is treacherous since she could not have adhered to the "Know Your Client" rule from those distances. Apparently, Wells Fargo hired this broker from UBS with or without checking out her record first.

- In another case, the claimant alleged unsuitable investments, unauthorized trades in mutual funds and Treasury securities and unsuitable use of leverage, from 2003-2008.
  - Damage amount requested - $1,318,842.
  - Settlement amount - $175,000.

  Advisor commented: "All of the allegations against me were false and I intended to vigorously defend myself at the ar-bitration. However, UBS alone decided to settle this matter to avoid further costs of litigation. I was not asked about the settlement nor was I asked to contribute to the settlement."[9]

- In another case, clients alleged that the Advisor recommended unsuitable investments. Time period 2001-2002.
  - Damage amount requested - $243,000.
  - Settlement amount - $75,000.
- In another case, claimant, who apparently never had an account with Wells Fargo Advisors, alleged that investment recommen-dations were misrepresented and unsuitable.
  - Settlement amount - $125,000.

- In the Wells Fargo Arlington, Virginia Office, customer alleged unauthorized trading, alleged unsuitability.
  - Damage amount requested - $239,650.
  - Damages granted - $51,250.

- In the Dallas, Texas office, client stated that her investments in mutual funds were unsuitable based on her risk tolerance and time horizon. She stated that the Advisor disregarded her needs. Compensatory damages not specified.
  - Settlement amount - $2,630.07

- In the Wells Fargo Eastchester, NY office, several bank customers alleged that bank accounts had been opened for them without their authorization.
  Advisor commented: "These allegations are false. When management accused me of these allegations, I was never provided the names of the customers or the ability to furnish signed paperwork to prove my innocence. Since then there has been no legal or regulatory action taken."[10]

- In the Bensalem, Pennsylvania office, four bank customers alleged that credit cards had been ordered for them but they had not requested them.
  - Financial Advisor was discharged.

- In another office, a complaint alleged that at the time the account was transferred in, the customer who confirmed the objective of "tax neutrality" to Advisor and that he never advised the customer that a large capital gain was incurred despite the fact that the account incurred a capital gain of $174,224.
  Advisor commented: "The parties named in the alleged

complaint have been misidentified. At the time the 'customer' elected to change money managers. I was not the broker of record. I had no involvement with the selection or recommendation of the investments or managers."[11]

* Other cases:

1. Allegations – suitability and unauthorized trades:
   o   Damage amount requested - $54,000.
   o   Result – customer settled.
2. Damage amount requested - $229,376.
   o   Settlement amount - $4,000.
3. Allegations – Misrepresentation.
   o   Damage amount requested - $13,286.17.
   o   Claim was denied.

• In the Langhorne, Pennsylvania office, allegations were made that the Advisor was in violation of Wachovia Bank's policies and procedures: opening accounts without client knowledge.
   o   Advisor was discharged.

Wells Fargo's brass did make a startling change in its compensation to Advisors. At first, it was announced that there would be "minimal changes for 2017,"[12] according to a conference call. But one alert Advisor who was on the call noted that bonuses for the sale of banking and lending products had been removed from the company's payout grid.

Typically, Wells Fargo Advisors could make between $2,000 and $100,000 in deferred compensation annually depending on how they grew their lending business.

One of the banking products that did undergo a profound change resulted in one of its largest customers to call it quits. Participants in TaxaSaver, a supplemental retirement plan for around 240,000 state employees and elected officials in Texas, were stunned by the changes and unhappy with the bank's new investment strategy and how it handled the transaction. Wells Fargo notified investors in April, 2007 that its target-date funds would become more aggressive and that it would seek better returns purchasing junk bonds, stocks in emerging markets and derivatives including credit default swaps, a big difference from the conservative investment strategy for which the funds were known. The retirement plan administrator asked Wells Fargo for more time over and above the 90 days to seek another manager but the request was denied. Ending a ten-year relationship, TaxaSaver pulled out more than $600 million.

A Colorado-based retirement plan for more than 4,000 plumbers and pipe-fitters also pulled its money from the Wells Fargo funds, citing the "unproven nature and significance"[13] of Wells Fargo's changes. "It was a big surprise," said Georgina Bouton, assistant director of benefit contracts. "What Wells Fargo wanted to do contradicted why we picked them in the first place. I'm unhappy with the lack of professionalism at Wells Fargo and how this was conducted."[14]

Wells Fargo explained that it needed to increase risk to generate more income for investors, and recognized that some customers are unhappy. Fredrik Axsater, the head of strategic business segments at Wells Fargo Asset Management, admitted that "if the client is disappointed, then we're disappointed. In our mind, the client is always right."[15]

"Investor needs have changed and evolved," Axsater explained. "We live longer. Life expectancy has extended. Retirement patterns have changed."[16]

They truly have changed for a lucky group of Wells Fargo employees in one of its San Jose, California branches. That's luck with a capital "L." In August, 2018, eleven coworkers pitched $2 each into an office pool and won the $543 million Mega Millions jackpot, the largest prize in California lottery history. After taxes, each participant would take home an estimated $19 million. The workers, ranging in age from 21 to 60, decided to take the next day, Saturday, off. A sign on the locked doors of the branch in a strip mall read: "This branch is closed."

Befuddled customers peered through the glass at clean desks, empty plastic chairs and an idle coffee machine, then celebrated the news, despite the inconvenience. They described the employees as polite and hard-working. They gave help to a handicapped customer, offering a chair and extra attention. "They're such down-to-earth people. It gives me chills,"[17] said customer Suzette Melegrito. "Wow, just wow," said another customer, returning her wallet to her purse. She then set off to find an ATM.

CHAPTER 8

HAVE TO USE THE BATHROOM? TOUGH LUCK

A former Wells Fargo employee, Nathan Todd Davis, stated at a California State Assembly hearing on the fake account scandal that he filed 50 ethics complaints during his ten years of employment but nothing was ever done. "I've been harassed, intimidated, written up and denied bathroom breaks,"[1] asserted Davis who drove 350 miles from his home to speak at the hearing. He directed his complaints to David Galasso, a senior Wells Fargo executive who was filling in at the hearing for CEO John Stumpf.

"The sales culture at Wells Fargo needs to be picked apart," he said, standing at the podium but looking to his right to address Galasso. Davis estimated that almost two-thirds of employees "cheat the system" due to unreasonable sales pressure. After a decade at Wells Fargo, he said he was fired for being "90 seconds late to work. The real problem was that he never made it to management because I don't cheat."[2] The bank declined to comment on the allegations, but said in a statement that it tries to make every employee "feel valued, rewarded and recognized."[3]

In order to achieve unrealistic sales goals, supervisors apparently threatened salespeople. One former employee interviewed by CNN reported: "I had managers in my face yelling at me. The sales pressure from management was unbearable."[4] Another former employee interviewed told the *L.A. Times* in 2013: "We were constantly told we would end up working for McDonald's. If we did not make the sales quotas… we had to stay for what felt like after-school detention, or report to a call session on Saturdays."[5] At some branches, not enough customers walked in the door, or residents were too poor to need more than a few banking products. A former branch manager said employees talked a homeless woman into opening six checking and savings accounts with fees totaling $39 a month. Bank leaders called overall quotas "50/50 plans" because they figured only half the regions could meet them. Yet no excuses were tolerated. You met the quotas or paid a price. An investigation found a branch manager who had a teenage daughter with twenty-four accounts, an adult daughter with eighteen accounts, a husband with twenty-one accounts, a brother with fourteen accounts, and a father with four accounts. A subsequent lawsuit against Wells Fargo alleged that "employees who failed to resort to illegal tactics were either demoted or fired."[6]

The problem is it can take years to get Congress and regulators to listen to whistleblowers like Davis. Finally, Congress has recognized and created both strong whistleblower anti-retaliation provisions and laws that provide financial incentives to those who step forward. For bank employees, the award provisions available for bank employees is the Financial Institutions Reform, Recovery and Enforcement Act (FIRREA) and the Financial Institutions Anti- Fraud Enforcement Act (FIAFEA). These laws allow whistleblowers to be awarded a percentage of whatever gets collected from banks, bank officers and third parties involved in banking fraud. These awards are capped at $1.6 million and the process to collect is fairly complex but with the right lawyer, the process becomes painless and easy. It doesn't make sense to pass legislation that gives an incentive to a whistleblower to come forward only to make it difficult to collect. What's the reasoning behind this?

There is one big exception and that is, if the government suffers a loss because a banking institution commits fraud and the government ends up on the wrong side of this mischief, the Federal False Claims Act FFCA) can pay even bigger awards, up to 30% of whatever the government collects from the wrongdoer with no cap or limit. As an example, one whistleblower was awarded over $50 million. Denying bathroom breaks to a bank employee who alerts management about identity theft or fake accounts turn conscientious employees into whistleblowers.

CEO Tim Sloan acknowledged in a speech that the bank bungled the initial response to the fake account scandal. "Many felt we blamed our team members. That one still hurts, and I am committed to rectifying it."[7] The bank eliminated the controversial sales goals and Sloan said Wells Fargo planned to introduce a new performance plan for retail bankers on "customer service, growth and risk management."[8]

One fraud investigator, who was a big critic of the bank, said things have started looking better. She said co-workers in the online customer service unit were less stressed due to the removal of the tough sales goals. "They can just concentrate on assisting the customer instead of having to sell something on every call."[9]

Not so for a Wells Fargo employee who worked in a California call center. She said things have actually gotten worse. She said her group was recently told not to use the restroom outside of scheduled breaks without a doctor's note. "The new CEO has no impact here in the trenches. People here are angry… feeling very dehumanized. Wells Fargo can give $120 million to a crooked CEO—but won't allow us to pee."[10]

The issue of workers being denied bathroom breaks was a troubling one that came up often during conversations between employees and CNNMoney. It's unclear how widespread the problem was, but former and current employees said it's resulted in stomach-related ailments in the past. A Wells Fargo spokeswoman said the bank complies with all applicable state and local laws. She said the bank is "investigating" the new claim from the employee about being denied bathroom breaks. "If we find it to be true, it is completely unacceptable and we will take immediate action."[11]

Sloan called it "disturbing to hear claims of retaliation against our team members." He said Wells Fargo was doing a "thorough review"[12] of its ethics line process. But letting his employees feel comfortable about using the hotline will not come easily, given the alarming allegations. Several current employees said they are still scared there will be negative repercussions if they blow the whistle. An employee who worked on auto loans said: "If and when we do speak up, it's disregarded. They will twist what you say to make it seem like you're crazy."[13]

Sloan delivered a companywide address on October 25, 2016 to 1,200 who were in attendance plus the thousands across the country who were watching on TeamTV and via a webcast. "My primary objective is to restore trust in Wells Fargo – restore pride in our company and mission. That may seem like a long ways off today, but I promise you we will."

"Things went wrong. Problems need to be fixed. Customers and team members were harmed and need to be cared for. And a better and stronger Wells Fargo must emerge out of all of this. Next year, we'll introduce a new performance plan for retail bankers that will be based on customer service, growth, and risk management. Our goal: We want nothing to get in the way of doing what is right for customers. We want to satisfy our customers' financial needs and help them succeed financially. This is why Wells Fargo exists. If our customers don't succeed, we don't."[14]

What drastic action could Congress take to punish Wells Fargo for all its sins even though new management is promising to make amends? Of the $190 million fine imposed as part of the settlement over the fake accounts, $185 million went to the federal government and only $5 million was to be divided among customers who were wrongfully charged maintenance fees.

A powerful Democrat in Congress felt regulators should consider shutting the banking giant down for abusing the trust of millions of its customer. Maxine Waters on the House Financial Services Committee, issued a thirty-eight-page report slamming regulators for failing to punish the bank more severely. The report, prepared by the Democratic staff of the committee, described Wells Fargo as a repeat offender for, among other things, opening as many as 3.5 million potentially fake accounts, forcing up to 570,000 borrowers into unneeded auto insurance and allegedly discriminating in mortgage lending. "When a megabank has engaged in a pattern of extensive violations of law that harms millions of consumers, like Wells Fargo has," the report said, "it should not be allowed to continue to operate within our nation's banking system."[15]

The report argued that regulators should have considered harsher penalties: shutting down problem areas of Wells Fargo, removing executives and directors, banning personnel from working in the industry, revoking the bank's national charter, or even winding down the bank entirely. Senator Elizabeth Warren has repeatedly urged the Federal Reserve to exercise its power to remove most of Wells Fargo's board for providing poor oversight. Fed chief Janet Yellen called Wells Fargo's behavior "egregious and unacceptable"[16] and said the central bank was considering whether more punishments were needed.

CHAPTER 9

OLD CEO TAKES AN EXIT HIKE – NEW CEO TAKES A PAY HIKE

"You've shown gutless leadership. You should resign. You should be criminally investigated, return every nickel made during the scam, and face DOJ/SEC investigation" shouted Senator Elizabeth Warren at CEO John Stumpf in a Washington Senate hearing. She pointed out that Wells Fargo "set lofty sales targets for employees and encouraged them to push customers to sign up for more and more accounts and when it all blew up, you kept your job, and your multi-multimillion-dollar bonuses, and you went on television to blame thousands of $12-an-hour employees who were just trying to meet cross-sell quotas that made you rich. A bank teller would face criminal charges and a prison sentence for stealing a handful of twenties from the cash drawer. A bank CEO should not be able to oversee a massive fraud and simply walk away to enjoy his millions in retirement."[1]

Senator Robert Menendez called the bank's sales and management culture and its move to terminate thousands of staffers while simultaneously defending senior executives "despicable." "I am personally appalled by the size, the scope, the duration and the impact of the scandal, and I must say I am shocked and incredibly disappointed by the response of Wells Fargo's corporate executives. You and your chief financial officer have taken to the press and laid the blame squarely on low-paid retail bank employees, and while I don't excuse what they did by any stretch of the imagination, I find that despicable."[2]

While he said he was "deeply sorry" and insisting there was no "scheme"[3] to scam customers, Stumpf struggled at times to answer lawmakers' questions and often gave the impression he wasn't fully in charge of the company. I wonder how he was NOT aware of what was going on. He was the chief on duty during the whole mess. I got the impression he was startled by being in the predicament in which he found himself and didn't know what to make of the whole thing. To him, the whole scene must have been a big shock and an embarrassment. He looked as if he was surprised as to why he was there. After all, he was the kingpin of this hugely successful operation for many years and he must have wondered why he was being grilled. When he raised his heavily bandaged right hand to take the oath, it looked like he was in a fight, but it was revealed he hurt it playing with his grandchildren. He was in a fight all right, not with his grandchildren, but in a fight to save his name and reputation. He lost.

During his testimony on Capitol Hill, he recalled hearing about the fake sales problems for the first time "in the summer/fall timeframe" of 2013. Not so, according to a Board of Directors' report that said he was notified of this in 2002 at one of the Colorado branches, which led to a "mass termination" of bank employees. Almost an entire branch was involved in issuing debit cards without customer consent to hit sales targets. The report added that similar incidents occurred "sporadically" over the next ten years. [4]

In 2004, the bank's internal investigations division noted an increase in "gaming" cases—defined as the manipulation and/or misrepresentation of sales to receive compensation or meet sales goals—from 63 in 2000 to a projected 680 in 2014. It produced a memo noting a similar increase in terminations from 21 in 2000 to a projected 223 in 2004. The memo recommended reducing or eliminating sales goals for employees, and removing the threat of dismissal if goals were not met. It was copied to the chief auditor and a senior in-house employment lawyer among other senior people. No action was taken. [5]

How could John Stumpf not be aware of what was going on?

Under a sales initiative which began in 2003, bankers were encouraged to start each year strongly, drawing up a hit lists of friends and family members who could be turned into customers. The campaign, known as "Jump into January,"[6] resulted in increased employee turnover and, in some areas, no paid time-off or training.

The big champion, Shelley Friedman, regional president in Los Angeles until 2009, then lead regional president in Florida until 2013, had employees "running the gauntlet." District managers would dress up in themed costumes before running down a line to a whiteboard to report the number of their sales. Pam Conboy, another regional manager, found a way of extending the campaign throughout the year ala "Fly into February, March into March," etc.[7]

Jeffrey Sonnenfeld, an authority on corporate governance at the Yale School of Management, said Stumpf proved to be a "deer caught in the headlights with a tin ear in understanding, addressing, and communicating the problem."[8] It is ironic that in a 2015 *Fortune* interview he called himself the "keeper of our company's culture."[9] And what culture would that be? Having his workers being fired for calling the so-called ethics hotline complaining about improper sales tactics?

Stumpf was named Morningstar's CEO of the year in 2015. The company applauded him for "shunning activities that put profits ahead of customers."[10] Where did they come up with that one? Looks like they didn't do their homework or were out to lunch when they should have been eating at their desks.

Senator Warren certainly made an impression on Stumpf, and he took her advice to retire. A person familiar with the matter said that Stumpf made that decision, which was welcomed by the board on October 12, 2016. "I am grateful for the opportunity to have led Wells Fargo," Stumpf said. "While I have been deeply committed and focused on managing the company through this period, I have decided it is best for the company that I step aside." He said he takes "full responsibility" for "all unethical sales practices."[11]

Four years later, he was bestowed with the dishonor of receiving a lifetime ban from the banking industry.

Robert Weissman, president of the activist group Public Citizen, put it this way: "The retirement is essentially an admission of wrongdoing that only reinforces the need to continue tough criminal investigations"[12] of Stumpf and other top executives. Jaret Seiberg, a managing director at Cowen and Company, said in 2016, his firm saw the executive shakeup as a "positive move," but noted the scandal is not over. "We continue to expect that Wells Fargo will be bogged down in this controversy for the next two years."[13]

On April 20, 2018, the company announced a settlement with the Office of the Comptroller of the Currency (OCC) and Consumer Financial Protection Bureau CFPB) to pay $1 billion in total civil money penalties. The fine is more than twice the amount of fines levied by the CFPB in its first twelve months of operation and the largest fine and second-largest enforcement action taken by the CFPB. Wells Fargo would also make full restitution to all of its victims and $50 million to the City and County of Los Angeles. To make matters worse, a number of states, including California, Ohio, and Illinois, and the cities of Seattle and Chicago, have suspended doing business with the bank. A study released in October of 2016 showed that it stood to lose $99 billion in deposits, $4 billion in revenue, and 30% of its customer base as a result of the scandal.

Stumpf and his cohorts must have thought that the penalty was "immaterial"[14] from a technical accounting standpoint. But the scandal had been going on for five years, two million customers' accounts had been affected and more than 5,300 employees had been fired. But no senior executives had been terminated. On the contrary, the executive who ran the retail unit where the shenanigans had occurred was scheduled for a "retirement" complete with a $128 million get away package. Yikes!

Before the fake account scandal was announced, Stumpf had been widely lauded as an everyday guy from middle America. One of eleven kids, he grew up getting his hands dirty working on his family's dairy farm in Minnesota. He shared a bed with two of his brothers until he was eighteen. He woke up at 4:30 every morning to milk cows and smelled like Holstein Friesian cattle. "We had tough times, and we were poor, but we got through it because we were in it together"[15] he told *Fortune*. After college, he worked as a repo man. "What got John most excited was talking about his days as a repo man," said an investor who knew him well. "He had these vivid stories of repossessing cars while another guy would be the lookout guy."[16] It seems to this author that these are just the right ingredients for showing the world that, despite all his hardships, there is still money to be made out there whether it's the right way or the shady way. It is obvious to me he took the latter path which ultimately led to his demise. But how could this have gone on so long without his knowledge? Perhaps, it was his stoic belief that Wells was a "community banker" that could do no wrong.

A day after *The New York Time's* Andrew Ross Sorkin dedicated his column to "pervasive sham deals at Wells Fargo,"[17] and a day before Stumpf was scheduled to appear before the Senate hearing, he was at the wrong end of a media interview. *The Wall Street Journal* characterized him as blaming the fired employees. Warren Buffett, whose Berkshire Hathaway was Wells Fargo's major shareholder, told Stumpf that he had underestimated the significance of the scandal and Stumpf replied that he no longer did. [18]

Anticipating a more hostile environment at his upcoming second hearing before a House panel, he and his team came up with a proposal that would show the representatives that he and his cohorts were serious about the company's misdeeds. They would claw back $41 million of his compensation. However, some clever journalists quickly identified that nothing was actually being clawed back but, instead, the $41 million would be eliminated from future compensation. Stumpf and his cronies couldn't even get that right.

After a six-month investigation, Wells Fargo's independent board of directors initiated corporate pay clawbacks that totaled some of the largest in history. Stumpf acknowledged that he made significant mistakes and helped create a culture that resulted in various abuses. According to executive compensation firm Equitar, Stumpf's total pay from 2011-2016 was $286 million, meaning that he would have forfeited 24% of his pay for that period. According to the board, Stumpf was made aware of the bank's systemic nature of sales practice problems starting in 2012, and was first aware of specific cases as early as 2002 and did not initiate any follow-up investigation or inquiry into the problem until 2015.

Sonnenfield thought Stumpf "should be subject to more clawbacks" and that part of his $107 million of stock should be clawed back if the shares were awarded for reaching targets of cross-selling, an industry-wide practice of selling customers multiple products, which is behind the fake accounts scandal.[19]

One of the main accusations was an unwillingness to criticize former Community Bank unit head Carrie Tolstedt, whom he once praised as being "the best banker in America."[20] Stumpf was hesitant to criticize Tolstedt and, ultimately, hesitant to terminate her, even after the lead independent director and the Chair of the Risk Committee suggested that he do so in 2015, according to details in a report. The board singled her out for far more criticism than anyone else for "creating the problems and failing to address them even when confronted with evidence that it led to low-quality sales and improper sales practices." She was "obsessed" with control, especially over negative information about the bank, and extremely reluctant to make changes.[21] She was terminated for cause and gave up an additional $47.3 million of pay on top of the $19 million the year before. Community Bank was Wells Fargo's consumer banking unit.

The report went on to say that current Wells Fargo CEO Tim Sloan's "direct involvement with the sales practices issue was limited"[22] until he became president and chief operating officer. At that point Tolstedt began reporting directly to him instead of to Stumpf. Sloan was credited with deciding to end her tenure, which Stumpf refused to do.

One email stood out that highlighted Stumpf's unwillingness to even acknowledge the scale of the problem his company faced. In an email to Sloan on May 17, 2015, after the company was notified that a lawsuit was filed against the bank by the city attorney of Los Angeles, Stumpf wrote: "I have worked over the weekend with Carrie [Tolstedt] on the LA issue; I really feel for Carrie and her team. We do such a good job in this area. I will fight this one to the finish. Do you know only around 1% of our people lose their jobs [for] gaming the system, and about 2/3 of those are for gaming the monitoring of the system, i.e. changing phone numbers, etc. Nothing could be further from the truth on forcing products on customers. In any case, right will win and we are right. Did some things wrong—you bet and that is called life. This is not systemic."[23]

So, how was Sloan rewarded for his ascending to the throne? He received $17.4 million in compensation, a roughly 36% hike from the previous year. During 2017, Sloan's first full year as chief executive, his base salary was $2.4 million and a $15 million bonus in the form of shares based on the company's long-term performance. According to the bank's annual proxy statement, Wells Fargo's board agreed with Sloan's request that he not receive a cash bonus based on his ultimate responsibility, as CEO, for the company's performance, which included significant but incomplete progress on addressing compliance and operational risk-management issues. It should be noted that although his total compensation was the lowest among chief executives of the largest U.S. banks, it was 291 times as much as the median compensation of all other Wells Fargo employees as noted in the filing. In 2016, Sloan was awarded $12,829,502 in compensation and he and other top Wells executives did not receive cash bonuses for that year. No surprise here. If they had, it would have been a travesty and a disgrace on top of what turned out to be a travesty and a disgrace.

CHAPTER 10

TO BANK OR NOT TO BANK? THAT IS THE QUESTION

But what is the answer? It depends on why you use your bank. For making deposits? For cashing checks? For buying CDs? For making investments? For renting a safe deposit box? For taking out a loan? For some, none or for all?

I remember in the late 60's and early 70's, people couldn't get enough of the banking trends. I knew someone who made a fortune seeking out locations and arranging for the construction of many branches. And he didn't even work for a particular bank. He free-lanced and developed a reputation as a premier "bank locator." And wouldn't you know it? Soon, there popped up the proverbial "bank on every corner." They were everywhere.

The problem was there weren't enough customers to go around and spreading the wealth was getting harder to come by. Soon, banks were competing with one another by offering gifts ranging from toasters, microwaves, even TV's just to get you in the door to open up an account. When that got "old," another banking ploy hit the street but, this time, it was through the mail. Bankers were offering hundreds of dollars if you opened up a checking account. The catch was you had to agree to have a certain amount of direct deposits flow into those accounts over a certain period of time. I was one of those who fell for this and, you guessed it, it was with Wells Fargo. I agreed to a direct deposit of at least $300 over a three-month period from funds that would normally go directly into one of my checking accounts. When that didn't happen, my account was closed and I was charged $25 for closing the account. I guess I didn't read the fine print. I appealed the decision but got nowhere.

In the mid-70's, a new phenomenon hit the investment world and it would revolutionize the manner in which mutual funds would offer non-risk accounts. It was called a "money market" fund. Now, banks were facing competition the likes of which they had never seen before. Prior to this, if an investor wanted to park some money between investments, the funds were left at the brokerage firm or deposited in a savings or checking account. Now, the investor could open up a money market account and transfer funds into the brokerage account when needed. It became a trillion-dollar industry overnight. As of April 30, 2018, $3.015 trillion was held in money market funds most of which (over $2 trillion) was invested in government and Treasury securities. There is a big difference though between what banks, credit unions and mutual funds offer. The latter is not FDIC (Federal Deposit Insurance Corporation) or NCUA (National Credit Union Association) insured. So, the banks and credit unions have a big advantage in that regard. But for most investors, parking funds in a money market fund which offers government or tax-exempt income is a big advantage even if they aren't insured.

So, what were the banks to do? They started putting ATM machines outside every branch. In this way, they could still maintain their customers who didn't necessarily have to enter the bank to withdraw funds. But a funny thing happened. Since fewer customers were going inside the branch, the banks had a problem and it was called "personnel." They didn't need as many workers inside, so they began to lay off people. This irritated customers who had to wait on lines to transact their business inside the branch, which usually consisted of depositing and/or cashing checks besides applying for loans. I began to bring reading material into my bank while waiting on line just like I did and still do when I enter a post office.

With the proliferation of money market funds offered by mutual funds and brokerage firms, what was the hapless banking industry to do? Why not compete in their own backyard. So, they started to offer investment products, insurance and, in the case of Wells Fargo, had a special division to market these investments as described in Chapter 6. What were the rank and file of employees, the so-called "team members" left to do? We saw the results very clearly—one scandal after another. Play the game or get ejected.

On January 12, 2018, a headline screamed:

"Wells Fargo plans to close 900 branches"

...by the end of 2020. The bank said that the acceleration of closures was due to customers' online and mobile banking and not the result of its scandals. Tim Sloan said, "They still want to come into our branches but they're also assessing us online, on mobile, through ATMs and over the phone." He explained that the pace of branch closures may fluctuate based on how customers respond. "We may increase, or we may decrease, who knows."[1] However, there are Wall Street analysts who are also blaming rising legal and compliance costs to clean up the mess. UBS analyst Saul Martinez wrote that he had long expected the "scandal was likely to be a catalyst for a more aggressive focus on expenses."[2] Wells Fargo said it's part of a broader plan to save about $2 billion a year by the end of 2019.

Mike Mayo, a bank analyst at CSLA, told CNN Money that he believes Wells Fargo will need to ultimately close 1,000 branches. He argued that the bank's massive branch network may have helped fuel the fake account scandal. He believed the need to justify the branch costs "could have contributed to pressure on staff to sell more."[3] A UBS analyst found that more than 40% of Wells Fargo branches lie within a five-minute drive of another branch. It said that's among the highest "cannibalization"[4] ratios of any of the big banks.

"Based on our current assumptions regarding consumer channel behavior and our own technology advances as well as other factors, we can see our total branch network declining to approximately 5,000 by the end of 2020," said John Shrewsberry, CFO of Wells Fargo. As of September 30, 2017, the bank had 6,082 branches in the U.S. "Branches play an important part in servicing our customers and we will have as many branches as our customers want for as long as they want them,"[5] Shrewsberry pointed out.

In 2018, it was scheduled to close its flagship location in downtown Charleston, South Carolina and two others in the state. Wells Fargo was the largest bank operating in the state based on its nearly 150 branches and more than $17 billion in deposits, according to the most recent federal data as of July of that year. The branch at Meeting and Market Streets, is situated at a prominent corner in the city's tourist and commercial district. Jim Lawrence, regional president, said the decision to close it was driven by "changes in customer behavior in the downtown Charleston area. Customers are saying to us they want to do business in a different way. We're trying to respond appropriately in giving them the tools and resources they want."[6]

What are they and how are they affecting the world of banking to which we've been accustomed in the past? Surely, mobile banking has been playing a bigger part as is online banking. Remember land lines for telephone usage? They're a thing of the past. Surely, iPhones and smart phones are the thing of the present and future. They have revolutionized the way we communicate. So, the need to visit your local branch has diminished dramatically and the need to hold on to that real estate on which it sits has become more costly to support. I went into my local cell phone store to purchase a new one and was told I had to make an appointment. They were booked for the day. From there, I went into my local bank branch. There were two tellers plus a manager with just one customer.

In 2017, JPMorgan Chase had 5,130 branches in twenty-three states and intended to expand into 15-20 new markets in several new states over the next five years including its first-ever in the Washington, DC area as part of a regional expansion that will bring seventy branch offices to the District, Maryland and Virginia by 2023, an area where it didn't have the exposure it wanted. In 2014, it had 5,600 branches. The company does have a presence in the region through JPMorgan Private Bank, a wealth management subsidiary. It says there are about 2 million customers who use its services without ever seeing a teller. But banking analysts say there remains a pool of customers who are more comfortable handling basic transactions in a branch. When big banks invest in new locations, "they are looking for opportunity," said Kenneth Leon, an equity analyst at CFRA Research. "There is part of the population that is interested in physical banking."[7]

In July, 2018, I received a letter from my bank stating it was planning on closing my local branch. "We don't take closing a branch lightly," the letter said. But with keeping costs under control, it decided to shut its doors. I can see why. It's rare that I see more than one person at the teller's window other than myself. The bank has another branch a half mile away. When I do visit that branch, again it's rare that I see more than one other customer. I was surprised when I saw that other branch for the first time. I didn't understand the reasoning behind having two branches so close to one another. I would think they would have taken opening another branch more than lightly. They must have had a reason for doing so. I, for one, just don't get it.

Banks shed more than 1,700 branches in the twelve months ending June, 2017, the biggest decline on record. The number of branches fell again in the second half of 2017. These would add to the thousands of locations closed following the financial crisis of 2008, the longest stretch of closures since the Great Depression.

Following is a list of those banks which closed the most branch locations (net) in 2017:

Wells Fargo –	194
JPMorgan Chase –	137
The Huntington National Bank –	134
First-Citizens Bank & Trust Co. –	127
Bank of America –	119
SunTrust Bank –	119
KeyBank –	112
PNC Bank –	109
Branch Banking and Trust Co. (BB&T) –	92
Capital One –	73

In a 2015 national survey by the FDIC of unbanked and under-banked households, it was revealed that there were an estimated 24.5 million people in the U.S. who were underbanked. The biggest reason for avoiding banks was the fear of not having enough money to open an account (57.4%). An additional 10.9% reported that they simply did not trust banks or believed the fees were too high (9.4%). Unfortunately, one poor personal experience or second-hand story of a negative bank relationship can be the reason for some to dislike the banking system and avoid it altogether. The jury is still out as to how many customers either closed their accounts at Wells Fargo or simply left their accounts open but did business elsewhere.

CHAPTER 11

NEW PREXY QUITS

Someone once said, "The more that things change, the more they stay the same." This appeared to be the case with Wells Fargo as *Barron's* reported on March 11, 2019:

> "Big Problems Remain at Wells Fargo." Wait a minute – wasn't the top brass supposed to have taken major steps to stop the shenanigans? Newly appointed CEO & President Timothy Sloan pledged to do so when he took over from disgraced John Stumpf in 2016.

But apparently Sloan had had enough. In a surprise move, on March 28, 2019, he abruptly quit. This after 31 years at Wells. In a conference call with analysts, he admitted, "I could not keep myself in a position where I was becoming a distraction."[1] Senator Elizabeth Warren's reaction? "About damn time. He enabled Wells Fargo's massive fake account scam, got rich off it, and then helped cover it up."[2]

Sloan had defended his work repairing the bank's practices and culture but at a hearing before lawmakers, they attacked his record after learning that many employees felt they were under pressure to reach certain sales goals that executives had insisted were no longer in force. Also, Senators Warren and Sherrod Brown urged the Federal Reserve Board to keep restrictions on the Bank's growth in place until Sloan was replaced as its chief executive. "Recent reports provide more evidence that Wells Fargo is fundamentally broke, with a record of misconduct that has lasted for years," they wrote in a letter. "There is no evidence whatsoever that Mr. Sloan will fix these problems."[3] The Fed Chairman, Jerome H. Powell, acknowledged that Wells Fargo still had "a lot of work to do" improving its internal controls. "What happened at Wells Fargo really was a remarkable wide-spread series of breakdowns,"[4] he stated.

But a number of current and former employees told *The New York Times* they "remain under heavy pressure to squeeze extra money out of customers," which led to "bending or breaking internal rules to meet ambitious performance goals."[1] This is after aggressive sales targets that resulted in millions of unauthorized accounts and other problems were supposedly changed with added safeguards to make sure there wasn't a repetition of these schemes.

A former financial advisor said that she was pressured along with other brokers to "steer clients toward investments that would generate recurring fees for the bank," including in a case where "it was not in the client's best interest."[2] The advisor, Melissa Kinnard, quit and, shortly afterward, Wells "sent a letter to her clients, in her name, announcing that she would be teaming up with another Wells Fargo employee to handle their accounts." [3]

The letter incorrectly stated that she was still at Wells and endorsed the other employee. Despite Kinnard's repeated requests, Wells did not retract the letter. A Wells spokesman told *Barron's* that the letter was sent in error to nineteen clients who were subsequently contacted and given the correct information. Mary Mack, Wells Fargo's head of consumer banking, told *The Times* "Things have changed a lot."[4] But the company's internal blog was filled with "hundreds of angry comments about Wells' sales incentives, pay and ethics and leaders' doublespeak,"[5] wrote *The Times.* Sloan called the story "patently not true" and said the bank "disagrees with almost every single word in the article."[6] He was the subject before the House Financial Services Committee in March, 2019, and it appeared he couldn't dodge the bullet. The hearing was titled, "Holding Megabanks Accountable:

An Examination of Wells Fargo's Pattern of Consumer Abuses." After bringing up several cases where Wells ripped off vulnerable people, Chairwoman Maxine Waters summarized the bank's abuses by declaring: "What this long but impartial list makes clear is that Wells Fargo is a recidivist financial institution that creates widespread harms with a broad range of offenses."[7]

Sloan countered with the explanation that: "The past few years have taught us that our company does well by doing right. But doing right does not stop with simply repairing harm and rebuilding trust."[8] Waters snapped back: "With all of this experience and the length of time you've been there and the roles you have played, you have not been able to keep Wells Fargo out of trouble. You keep getting fined. Why should Wells Fargo continue to be the size that it is?"[9]

She was not satisfied with his answer that the culture of the company is changing and that there's a new "customer focus."[10] She suggested the bank should be downsized because it was too large to manage and urged the Office of the Comptroller of the Currency to replace senior executives and board members.

At a hearing before the House Financial Services Committee in March, 2019, entitled "Holding Megabanks Accountable: An Examination of Wells Fargo's Pattern of Consumer Abuses," Representative Katie Porter from California asked Sloan if his statements about customers being able to trust Wells Fargo "meant something to him. Are you lying to a federal judge, or are you lying to me and this Congress right now on whether we can rely on those statements?"[11] "Neither,"[12] Sloan responded.

Soon after the hearing, a spokesman for the OCC declared: "We continue to be disappointed with [Wells Fargo's] performance under our consent orders and its inability to execute effective corporate governance and a successful risk management program. We expect National Banks to treat their customers fairly, operate in a safe and sound manner and follow the rules of law."[13] It appeared to this observer that

Mr. Sloan's countenance during the hearing looked rather tired and/or maybe he was just plain disgusted with the whole thing.

> O-ho the Wells Fargo Wagon is a comin' down the street,
> Oh please let it not be for me!
> O-ho the Wells Fargo Wagon is a comin' down the street,
> Without a driver – oh how, oh how it could be?
> Oh-ho the Wells Fargo wagon is a comin' down the street,
> Oh, please let it pass my door!
> Oh-ho the Wells Fargo Wagon is a comin' down the street,
> I don't think I can take this anymore!

NOT SO SAFE SAFETY DEPOSIT BOXES

After writing eleven chapters of this book, I thought my goal was completed, which was to tell the reader and the world how Wells Fargo, a bank of such notoriety, could have sunk to an even more abysmal abyss. Not so. Just two weeks later, it was revealed that Wells Fargo was caught in yet another scandal.

Philip Poniz had collected unusual watches since he was a teenager in the 1960s in Poland. His hobby turned into his profession and, by the time he moved to New Jersey in the 80's, he had become an internationally known expert in the history and restoration of expensive timepieces. At first, he kept his collection in his house but as it grew, he wanted something secure, so in 1983, he signed a one-page lease agreement for a safe deposit box with First National State Bank of Edison in Highland Park, New Jersey.

Over the next few decades, the bank changed hands many times. First National became First Union, which was later sold to Wachovia, which was then bought by Wells Fargo. The vault remained the same. A foot-thick steel door sheltered cabinets filled with hundreds of stacked metal boxes each protected by two keys. The bank kept one and the customer held the other. Both were required to open a box.

In 1998, Poniz rented several additional boxes and separated a batch of personal effects – photographs, coins inherited from his grandfather and dozens of watches into a box number 105. Every time he opened it, he saw the accumulation of his life's work. Then, on April 7, 2014, he lifted the metal lid. The box was empty. "I thought my heart would fail."[1] At age 67, he still has a strong Polish accent and speaks English only carefully. Poniz struggled to find the right words to describe when he discovered his watches were missing. "I was devastated," he said. "I was never like that in my life before. I had never known that one can have a feeling like that."[2]

In the days after Poniz found the box empty, he began piecing together what had happened. Wells Fargo had apparently tried to evict another customer for not keeping up with payments, and bank employees had mistakenly removed his box instead. After drilling No. 105 open, the bank shipped its contents to a storage facility in North Carolina. When Poniz discovered the loss, Wells Fargo sent back everything that was in storage but, in the process, some items had vanished. New Jersey law requires a bank to bring in an independent notary when it opens and empties a safe deposit box and to place its contents in a sealed package signed by the notary. The disappearance of the watches and coins suggests that the bank didn't follow that law.

Jim Seitz, a bank spokesman, said, "Wells Fargo is reviewing the facts and circumstances of this case. We cannot comment further due to pending litigation."[3] One of the lawyers hired by Poniz said he pressed the bank to find the missing items and asked for a financial settlement.

Wells Fargo declined so Poniz sued in New Jersey's Superior Court. The bank sought to move the case to arbitration, which would keep the dispute out of the public record. This tends to favor companies over the individuals challenging them.

The two sides battled over that request for nearly two years until a judge ruled in November, 2018, that the case should remain in court, not in arbitration. The bank appealed, prolonging the dispute. Meanwhile, the lawsuit appeared nowhere near a resolution, and Poniz had already run up tens of thousands of dollars in legal fees. Craig Borgen, another lawyer representing Poniz, said, "The bank has spent a tremendous amount of resources and put them into defending the case, instead of stepping forward and saying, 'We made a mistake here, let's make it right.'"[4]

How could this happen? It seems that halfway up a different wall in the vault was another box 105 – the result of the bank's consolidation of several branches' safe deposit boxes into a single location and having kept the original number.

Bank employees got them mixed up and emptied the wrong one. They created an inventory that included ninety-two watches, but when employees in the bank's storage facility in North Carolina counted the items, they listed only eighty-five. Also missing were dozens of rare coins that were listed in the first inventory but not the second. According to Poniz, photographs and family documents also disappeared. Wells returned to him five watches that weren't his. "They were the wrong color, the wrong size – totally different from what I had," Poniz said. "I had no idea where they came from."[5]

The watches that vanished were the largest and most visually striking in his collection. There was a Tiffany watch that tracked the moon's phases on its gold dial and an early Breguet watch that was engraved with the coat of arms of the Duke of New Orleans. The highlight was a rare nineteenth century pocket watch with a face that was dotted with pearls and rubies that concealed a pop-up bird, slightly larger than a thumbnail, that twittered and sang. Such "singing" bird watches rarely come to market. One of them was sold at auction for $772,500 in 1999.

John North, a lawyer representing the bank, said at a court hearing: "There's no question that Wells Fargo drilled the box and took the contents out of it, put it in storage and then returned it. The underlying dispute is, was everything returned or not?"[6] In his six-page report with the Highland Park police, Poniz described the watches, coins, documents and other items that were gone. He estimated that their combined value was more than $10 million which would make it one of the largest safe deposit losses in U.S. history.

When cases do go to court, the bank often has the advantage. Lianna Saribekyan and her husband, Agassi Halajyan, leased a large safe deposit box at a Bank of America branch in 2012. They filled it with jewelry, gemstones, cash and family heirlooms that they wanted to keep safe while they renovated their home. They paid $246 for a one-year rental. Nine months later, Saribekyan returned to the branch only to discover that her box was gone.

The bank was closing and drilled open all of its safe deposit boxes. The bank said it sent multiple letters to customers about the branch closure.

Saribekyan said she never received them. When Bank of America retrieved her items from its storage depot, many were missing. The bank's own before-and-after inventories, written by employees, showed discrepancies, according to court records. Among the items that vanished, she said, were forty-four loose diamonds, a gold and diamond necklace, valuable coins and more than $24,000 in rare U.S. currency.

She sued the bank seeking $7.3 million. Bank of America tried to have the case dismissed, citing language in its lease agreement stating that the renter "assumes all risks" of leaving property in the box. But after a month-long trial, a jury awarded her $2.5 million for her lost items and an additional $2 million in punitive damages.

Bank of America challenged the verdict, arguing that any recovery should be restricted by the terms detailed in its rental contract which stated: "The bank's liability for any loss in connection with the box for whatever reason shall not exceed ten times the annual rent charged for the box."

The judge agreed and reduced the compensation for the lost items to $2,460 and the punitive damages to $150,000. "We were shocked, furious and in disbelief that such a thing could happen," Halajyan said. "The attorneys were throwing stupid counterarguments at us, asking, 'Why would you put so many valuables in the safe deposit box?' We were like, where else do you want us to put it? The word 'safe' is supposed to mean 'safe.'"[7]

A Bank of America spokeswoman declined to comment on the case. The company's restriction terms aren't unusual.

Wells Fargo's safe deposit contact caps the bank's liability at $500. Citigroup limits it to 500 times the box's annual rent and JPMorgan

Chase has a $25,000 ceiling on its liability. Banks typically argue and courts have in many cases agreed that customers are bound by the bank's most current terms, even if they leased their boxes years or even decades earlier.

No regulator formally tallies customer losses in safe deposit boxes but in legal filings and news reports, it is estimated that around 33,000 boxes a year are affected by accidents, natural disasters and thefts. The Office of the Comptroller of the Currency, the banking industry's main federal overseer, said it had no grounds to get involved. An agency spokesman, Bryan Hubbard, stated: "No provision of federal banking law expressly regulates safe deposit boxes."

Poniz wasn't alone. Another New Jersey resident had another problem with Wells Fargo. Syed Ali found himself at odds with the very security measures put in place to protect him when the bank blocked him from his own safe deposit box. Ali didn't have a driver's license and locked inside the box was the only other form of ID he had – a passport he needed to visit his ailing mother in India. "I have the key and I have a bank card from the bank and so many times previously—maybe twenty-five times—I got inside and nobody asked me for more identification. Now this time they didn't allow me to go in. I explained that my mother is in a very serious condition, but they said no."[8]

The next day, he returned with an attorney but it was no use. A few weeks later, his mother passed away and the safe deposit box remained under lock and key. No bank will allow customers access to safe deposit boxes without a form of ID, though Wells Fargo eventually relaxed its rules for Ali but it was too late.

In Charlotte, North Carolina, Arlando Henderson, a bank employee, had keys to the bank's vault and stole more than $88,000 with which he bought a 2019 Mercedes Benz by putting $20,000 down in cash. On at least eighteen occasions in 2019, he stole cash from deposits from the bank's vault and posted pictures of himself on social media holding stacks of cash. He certainly wasn't shy about his transgressions.

In another instance, a couple accused Bank of America of losing $17,000 worth of jewelry including family heirlooms and the gems the wife wore on her wedding day. She discovered her safe deposit box was empty when she opened it. She and her husband were shocked to find their valuables were gone and immediately filed a police report.

"I just got robbed from the bank, they just took my stuff." [9] she said with a shrug. The bank later told them it had drilled their box because it did not have on file account information such as the husband's social security number and birthdate. "They never notified us," the husband claimed.

Bank of America insisted it sent a notification letter in 2015, about a year before it drilled the box, but the couple insisted they never received the letter, and the bank could not provide evidence it was ever sent. The couple said the first letter received from the bank came two weeks after the box was discovered empty and months after the bank had drilled it.

As it turned out, Bank of America may have had the allegedly missing information all along. It had a copy of their original rental agreement, complete with all of the information.

The couple was even more shocked by the way the bank handled their precious items. After drilling the box, the bank shipped their nearly $100,000 worth of jewelry and irreplaceable possessions to a holding center and when they got them back, they were in a UPS box.

The bank's rental agreement said it may ship contents of a safe deposit uninsured.

When the couple opened the box, they were horrified to discover that bank employees had removed their delicate jewelry from its individual protective boxes and silk bags and thrown them all together which took an hour to untangle.

They said that several pieces were damaged or broken and, after untangling them, they discovered $17,000 was still missing. The couple spent the next two months trying to get answers from Bank of America, which finally reimbursed them for the jewelry that was lost.

A woman described a similar chain of events involving her safe deposit box that was also drilled into without warning and her valuables shipped back damaged.

The woman, Wendy Woo, said her jewelry was removed from individual protective jewelry bags and tangled together in a single plastic bag. She took photos of two family heirlooms that had been damaged in the shipment including a ring with a missing stone and a broken necklace. She spent the next several months trying to convince the bank to pay for repairs. The bank agreed to the repairs.

Bank of America said it drilled into her box because of a missing social security number of her mother's, a co-signer on the box, who had recently died. The bank claimed it sent Woo a letter requesting the information in 2015.

When asked to produce the letter, she said they never did send one. It finally did send an alleged copy of the letter but couldn't provide a delivery confirmation or proof of return service.

Another woman had to sue to get her items shipped back fully insured. Her safe deposit had been drilled into due to an allegedly missing social security number despite the fact that it was clearly written on her safe deposit rental agreement.

San Francisco attorney, Chris Land, said his clients had a similar story. However, in this case, instead of missing jewelry, the bank lost their original deed to real property in China. "They needed that deed to prove their ownership of the property. Without it, they were going to lose their property," he said.[10]

The bank said it drilled their safe deposit box due to missing personal information and claimed to have sent them a letter in 2015.

Like the others, Land said the couple never received the letter and the bank could not provide evidence that the notification was ever sent.

"There's no evidence of any registered or certified mail and the bank told my clients they no longer had this alleged letter," Land said.[11] However, Land did have a copy of the original safe deposit rental agreement, complete with the alleged missing information.

According to the OCC, banks may drill a box without permission due to a court order, search warrant, delinquent rental fees, requests from estate administrators or if a bank is closing a branch.

While nothing in federal regulations specifically authorizes a bank to drill a safe deposit box due to missing information, the rental agreement does specify that the bank can terminate a rental agreement for failure of any renter to provide proper identification upon request.

The OCC was repeatedly asked if it would take enforcement action against a bank for unlawfully or erroneously drilling a safe deposit box and/or losing its contents.

The agency declined to comment. It also wouldn't confirm whether it has ever taken action on behalf of a customer but, in response to a Freedom of Information Act request, it did provide statistics on safe deposit drilling complaints.

Wells Fargo led the list with 24%; Bank of America was close behind with 23%. The remaining 53% was divided among 60+ other federally regulated banks.

Safe deposit consultant, Dave McGuinn, says he's been hired as an expert witness on seventeen different cases involving big banks and notes that federal law does require banks to provide customers with adequate notice.

"Notification should be made by registered letter or a certified return receipt letter so the bank has proof that a notice was sent out,"[12] McGuinn explains.

He trains bank employees on proper safe deposit procedures. Bank of America says it does "notify customers by mail in accordance with the law well in advance to drilling a box and has protocols to verbally communicate the matter when customers come into the financial center to access their box."[13]

The bank would not comment on why these protocols were not followed in the above cases. Most customers don't realize that boxes are not insured unless they buy a separate policy from a third-party insurer or add a rider to a homeowner's policy. Many are also shocked to find out that under the rental agreement a bank's liability is limited.

An estimated 25 million safe deposit boxes are kept in the U.S. and they operate in a legal gray zone within the highly regulated banking industry. No federal laws govern the boxes and no rules require banks to compensate customers if their property is stolen or destroyed.

Every year, a few hundred customers report to authorities that valuable items—jewelry, diamonds, rare coins, art, memorabilia, cash –have disappeared from safe deposit boxes. Sometimes the fault lies with the customer who removes items and then forgets to return them. Others allow children or spouses to gain access to their boxes. But even when a bank is clearly at fault, customers rarely recover more than a small fraction of what they've lost, if anything.

McGuinn, the founder of Safe Deposit Specialists, states that, "the big banks fight tooth and nail, prolong and delay—whatever it takes to wear people down. The larger the claim, the more likely they are to battle it for years."[13]

Banks increasingly regard safe deposit boxes as more of a headache than they're worth. They're expensive to build, complicated to maintain and not very lucrative.

The four largest banks—JPMorgan Chase, Bank of America, Wells Fargo, and Citigroup—rarely install them in new branches. Capital One stopped renting out new boxes in 2016. A spokesman said that a dwindling number of customers wanted them. No doubt, the bank did not make them a priority since converting branches to the novel new format much like The Financial Store.

Jerry Pluard, the president of Safe Deposit Box Insurance Coverage, a Chicago firm that insures boxes says, "All of the major national banks would prefer to be out of the safe deposit box business. They view it as a legacy service that's not strategic to anything they do, and they've stopped putting any real focus or resources into it."[14]

The number of bank branches in the U.S. is steadily declining—down 10% in the last ten years and, as a result, safe deposit boxes are being relocated and sometimes misplaced.

A customer claims in a lawsuit that he lost gems and gold valued at half a million dollars from a large bank in Maryland that closed several branches and lost track of hundreds of boxes.

In Florida, a Chase customer accused the bank of losing her box and all of its contents worth more than $100,000. When she sued, a federal judge ruled that she waited too long to file her claim and decided in the bank's favor.

In California, a Wells Fargo customer said the bank accidentally re-rented her box; the diamond necklace and other jewels she had in it were never found.

Endnotes

Preface

1. Matt Eagan, "California blames Wells Fargo for 1,500 fake insurance policies," CNN BUSINESS, December 6, 2017.
2. Maggie McGrath, "Wells Fargo Fined $185 Million For Opening Accounts Without Customers' Knowledge, *Forbes*, September 8, 2016.
3. Ibid.
4. Ibid.

Chapter 1

1. Wells Fargo's 2010 Annual Report.
2. Matt Egan, "Workers tell Wells Fargo horror stories," CNN Money, September 9, 2016, 2.
3. Elizabeth C. Tippett, "How Wells Fargo Nudged Their Employees to Commit Fraud," The Decision Lab, November, 2016, 4.
4. Ibid, 5.
5. Wells Fargo Press Release, March 1, 2018.
6. "History of Wells Fargo," www wellsfargo.com, 1.
7. Ibid 2.
8. Wells Fargo Stories, October 25, 2016.

Chapter 2

1. W1. Wells Fargo's 2010 Annual Report.
2. Matt Egan, "Workers tell Wells Fargo horror stories," CNN Money, September 9, 2016, 2.

3. Elizabeth C. Tippett, "How Wells Fargo Nudged Their Employees to Commit Fraud," The Decision Lab, November, 2016, 4.

4. Ibid, 5.

5. Wells Fargo Press Release, March 1, 2018.

6. "History of Wells Fargo," www. wellsfargo.com,1.

7. Ibid, 2.

8. Wells Fargo Stories, October 25, 2016.

Chapter 3

1. Andrew Ross Sorkin, "Pervasive Sham Deals at Wells Fargo, and No One Noticed?", *The New York Times*, Dealbook, September 12, 2016.

2. Bill Chappell, "Wells Fargo Hit With $1 Billion in Fines Over Home and Auto Loan Abuses," npr.org., April 20, 2018.

3. James Rufus Koren, "Wells Fargo to pay $185 million settlement for 'outrageous' sales culture.", www.latimes.com/business, September 8, 2016, 2.

4. Ibid, 6.

5. Bloomberg, "Judge approves a $142-million settlement over the Wells Fargo accounts scandal, calling it 'rough justice'," latimes.org/business, May 30, 2018, 1.

6. Ibid, 3.

7. Matt Egan, "Wells Fargo isn't the only bank with fake accounts," CNN Money, June 6, 2018, 1.

8. Stacy Cowley, "Wells Fargo Finds 1.4 Million More Suspect Accounts," *The New York Times* Dealbook, August 31, 2017.

9. Ben Popken, "Wells Fargo hit with yet another lawsuit – for closing fraud victims accounts to avoid costs," NBC News, March 1, 2018.

10. Emily Flitter and Stacy Cowley, "Wells Fargo Accused of

Harming Fraud Victims by Closing Accounts," *The New York Times*, February 28, 2018.

11. Ibid.

12. Ibid.

13. Bloomberg, "The Wells Fargo Fake Accounts Scandal Just Got a lot Worse," *Fortune*, August 31, 2017.

Chapter 4

1. Emily Flitter, "The Former Khmer Rouge Slave Who Blew the Whistle on Wells Fargo," *The New York Times*, March 24, 2018, 2.

2. Ibid.

3. Ibid.

4. Ibid, 5.

5. Ibid, 6.

6. Ibid.

7. Ibid.

8. Ibid, 8.

9. Ibid.

10. Ibid, 9.

11. Ibid.

12. Ibid.

Chapter 5

1. Stacy Cowley, "'Lions Hunting Zebras': Ex-Wells Fargo Bankers Describe Abuses," *The New York Times*, October 20, 2016, DealBook, 1.

2. Ibid, 4.

3. Ibid, 5.

4. Ibid, 2.

5. Ibid, 3.

6. Ibid, 3.

7. Ibid, 4.
8. Ibid, 6.
9. Ibid, 3.
10. Matt Egan, "Wells Fargo sold dangerous investments it didn't understand, regulators say," CNN Money, October 16, 2017, 2.
11. Ibid.
12. James Rufus Koren, "Wells Fargo ordered to repay customers who lost money on complex securities," *The L.A. Times*, October 17, 2017, 4.

Chapter 6

1. Antoine Gara, "Another Disaster for Wells Fargo: Troubled Bank Admits Charging Unnecessary Auto Insurance," *Forbes*, July 28, 2017, 1.
2. Press Release: New York Statement from New York City Comptroller Scott M. Stringer on New Revelations of Mismanagement At Wells Fargo, 1.
3. Berkeley Lovelace, Jr.," Warren Buffett on Wells Fargo:' There's never just one cockroach in the kitchen'", www.cnbc.com, August 31, 2017, 1
4. William Watts, "Buffett says no surprise Wells Fargo forced to pay 'past sins'," www.marketwatch.com, February 26, 2018, 3.
5. Berkshire Hathaway's Annual Meeting.
6. William Watts, "Buffett says no surprise Wells Fargo forced to pay for 'past sins'," www.marketwatch.com. February 26, 2018.
7. Deirdre Fulton, "Wells Fargo CEO Steps Down but for Warren It's 'not real Accountability,'" Common Dreams, October 15, 2016.
8. Dan Freed: "RPT-Wells Fargo's new CEO faces immediate test," Reuters, October 13, 2016.
9. Megan Leonhardt," 'At Best Incompetent, at Worst Complicit'; Senators Slam Wells Fargo CEO Tim Sloan," Money, October 3, 2017.

10. Ibid.

11. Ibid.

12. Ibid.

13. Michael Corkery and Stacy Cowley, "Wells Fargo Warned Workers Against Sham Accounts, but 'They Needed a Paycheck'", *The New York Times*, September 16, 2016, 1.

14. Ibid, 3,

15. Kevin McCoy, "Wells Fargo faces new consumer lawsuit alleging improper mortgage fees," USA TODAY, September 5, 2017.

16. Ibid.

17. "How Wells Fargo's Cutthroat Corporate Culture Allegedly Drove Bankers to Fraud," *Vanity Fair*, May, 2017.

18. Ibid.

19. Ibid.

20. Ibid.

21. Ibid.

22. Ibid.

23. Ibid, 2.

24. Kevin McCoy, "Wells Fargo faces a new consumer lawsuit alleging improper mortgage fees," USA TODAY, September 5, 2017.

25. Ibid.

26. Ibid.

27. Ibid.

28. Matt Egan, "Wells Fargo hit homebuyers with fees to lock in interest rates, "CNN Money, October 4, 2017.

29. Adam Shell, "Wells Fargo plans to refund some mortgage customers," USA TODAY, October 4, 2017.

30. Matt Egan, "Wells Fargo accused of ripping off mom-and-pop shops," CNN Money, August 11, 2017, 1.

31. Ibid.

32. Ibid.

33. Ibid.

34. Ibid.

35. Peter Rudegeair, Emily Glazer and Coulter Jones, "Wells Fargo Fires Bankers Amid Probe of Dinner Receipts That Were Allegedly Doctored." *The Wall Street Journal*, August 30, 2018, 1.

Chapter 7

1. Martin Zimmerman, "Wells Fargo accused of securities fraud in state lawsuit," latimes.com, April 24, 2009, 1.

2. Ibid.

3. Matt Egan, "Wells Fargo sold dangerous investments it didn't understand, regulators say," CNN Money, October 16, 2017, 1.

4. Martin Zimmerman, "Wells Fargo accused of securities fraud in state lawsuit, latimes.com, April 24, 2009, 2.

5. Jackie Wattles, Ben Geier and Matt Egan, "Wells Fargo's 17-month Nightmare," CNN Money, February 5, 2018.

6. E. Scott Reckard and David Sabno, "Wells Fargo exec used Malibu Colony home lost by Madoff-duped couple, neighbors say," www.latimes.com, September 11, 2009.

7. Andrew Clark, "Wells Fargo fires executive who partied at repossessed Malibu mansion," *The Guardian*, September 15, 2019.

8. Ibid, 2.

9. FINRA Broker Check.

10. Ibid.

11. Ibid.

12. Tim McLaughlin, "Wells Fargo loses big client after dialing up risk in retirement funds, "Reuters Business News, February 1, 2018.

13. Ibid.

14. Ibid.

15. Bruce Kelly, "Wells Fargo eliminates bonuses for advisors selling banking products," www.investmentnews.com, December 15, 2016, 2.

16. Ibid, 6.

17. Lisa M. Krieger, "Surprise! Mega Millions winners take the day off Work," www.mercurynews.com, August 4, 2018.

Chapter 8

1. "No Bathroom Breaks, 'Unconscionable Behavior,' Says Former Wells Fargo Employee, "www.cutoday/info/Fresh-Today, November 7, 2016, 1

2. Ibid.

3. Ibid.

4. Ibid.

5. Matt Egan, "Workers tell Wells Fargo horror stories," CNN Money, September 9, 2016, 2.

6. Ibid.

7. E. Scott Reckard, "Wells Fargo's pressure-cooker sales culture

8. Camila Domonoske, "Ex-Wells Fargo Employees Sue, Allege They Were Punished for Not Breaking Law," The Two-Way: NPR, September 26,2016, 3.

9. Kaitlin Mulhere, "Wells Fargo is Eliminating Employee Sales Goals That Led to Fake-Account Scandal," *Money*, September 13, 2016, 1.

10. Matt Egan, "Inside Wells Fargo, workers say the mood is grim," *Money*, November 3, 2016, 1.

11. "Miserable Wells Fargo (BWF) employees say they've been de-nied bathroom breaks, thanks to its false account scandal." Quartz, 2.

12. Ibid.

13. Matt Egan, "Inside Wells Fargo, workers say the mood is grim," CNN Money, November 3, 2017, 3.

14. "Wells Fargo Stories, an online journal of working together. Inside the Stagecoach," stories.wf.com. October 25, 2016.

15. Matt Egan, "Top Democrat suggests Wells Fargo should be

shut down entirely," *CNN Money*, October 2, 2017,1.

16. Jeff Cox, "Yellen rips Wells Fargo scandal as 'egregious and un-acceptable,' www.cnbc.com, September 20, 2017, 1.

Chapter 9

1. Camila Domonoske, "Ex-Wells Fargo Employees Sue, Allege They Were Punished for Not Breaking Law," www.npr.org., September 26, 2016, 3.

2. Joe Marino, "Wells Fargo's 'fraud despicable,' senator tells bank CEO," CNBC, September 20, 2016.

3. Matt Egan, Jackie Wattles and Cristina Alesci, "Wells Fargo CEO is out," *CNN Money*, October 12, 2016.

4. "Five damning revelations from Wells Fargo report," *Financial Times*.

5. Ibid, 2.

6. Ibid.

7. Ibid.

8. Matt Egan, Jackie Wattles and Cristina Alesci, "Wells Fargo CEO is out, ", CNN Money, October 12, 2016.

9. Ibid.

10. John G. Stumpf, "How Wells Fargo's CEO built the team at the World's most valuable bank, "*Fortune*, July 24, 2015.

11. Paul Prendergrass, "How Wells Fargo's John Stumpf Crashed Himself," *Fortune*, October 14, 2016.

12. Matt Egan, Jackie Wattles and Cristina Alesci, "Wells Fargo CEO Is out," CNN Money, October 12, 2016.

13. Wilfred Frost, Dawn Giel, "Wells Fargo board slams former CEO Stumpf & Tolstedt, claws back $75 million, CNBC, April 10, 2017,1.

14. Ibid.

15. Ibid.

16. "How Wells Fargo's Cutthroat Corporate Culture Allegedly

Drove Bankers to Fraud," *Vanity Fair*, May, 2017, 12.

17. Jen Wieczner, "How Wells Fargo's Carrie Tolstedt Went from *Fortune's* Most Powerful Woman to Villain," *Fortune*, April 10, 2017.

18. Wilfred Frost, Dawn Giel, "Wells Fargo board slams former CEO Stumpf and Tolstedt, claws back $75 million, CNBC, April 10, 2017.

19. Matt Egan, "Wells Fargo CEO walks with $130 million," Money.cnn.com, October 13, 2016, 2.

20. Ron McLannahan and Alistair Gray, "Five damning revelations from Wells Fargo's report," *Financial Times*, April 10, 2017.

21. Jen Wieczner, "How Wells Fargo's Carrie Tolstedt Went from Fortune's Most Powerful Woman to Villain," *Fortune*, April 10, 2017.

22. Wilfred Frost, Dawn Giel, "Wells Fargo board slams former CEO Stumpf and Tolstedt, claws back $75 million, CNBC, April 10, 2017.

23. Ron McLannahan and Alistair Gray, "Five damning revelations from Wells Fargo's report," *Financial Times*, April 10, 2017.

Chapter 10

1. Matt Egan, "Wells Fargo is closing over 400 bank branches, "CNN Money, January 13, 2017, 3.

2. Ibid, 1.

3. Ibid, 2.

4. "Updated: Banks Closed Record Amount of Branches in 2017," www.friedmanrealestate.com, /news, 1.

5. Alistair Gray, Bloomberg, "Wells Fargo plans to close 900 branches despite $3.4bn tax boost," Wells Fargo January 12, 2018, 2.

6. John McDermott, "Wells Fargo closing its flagship Charleston branch. 2 other SC offices," www.Postandcourier.com/business, July 17, 2018, 2.

7. Aaron Gregg and Renae Merle, "Chase to open hundreds of

offices in US even as rivals abandon bank branches, *The Washington Post*, April 22, 2008.

Chapter 11

1. *Barron's*, "Report: Big Problems Remain at Wells Fargo," March 11, 2019, 1.
2. Ibid, 2.
3. Ibid.
4. Ibid.
5. Ibid.
6. Paul Blest, "Watching the Wells Fargo CEO Get Mauled in Congress for Hours Was So Satisfying," SPLINTER, March 12, 2019.
7. Ibid.
8. Ibid.
9. Ibid.
10. Ibid.
11. Ibid.
12. Ibid.
13. Rachel Louise Ensign and Andrew Ackerman, "*The Wall Street Journal*, March 13, 2019, 1.

Epilogue

1. Stacy Cowley, "Safe Deposit Boxes Aren't Safe," *The New York Times*, July 2019, 4.
2. Ibid, 5.
3. Ibid, 12.
4. Ibid, 15.
5. Ibid, 16.
6. Ibid, 14.
7. Ibid, 12.
8. Mandi Woodruff, "A New Jersey Man Claims Wells Fargo

Kept Him From Visiting His Dying Mother," *Business Insider*, May 10, 2012.

9. CBS San Francisco, "Customers Complain BofA is Drilling Safe Deposit Boxes and Losing Valuables," May 6, 2017.

10. Ibid. 7

11. Ibid.

12. Ibid.

13. Ibid

14. Stacy Cowley, "Safe Deposit Boxes Aren't Safe, The New York Times, July 19, 2019, 5.

15. CBS San Francisco, "Customers Complain BofA is Drilling Safe Deposit Boxes and Losing Valuables," May 6, 2017, 11.

.

CPSIA information can be obtained
at www.ICGtesting.com
Printed in the USA
FSHW020458100821
83952FS